My Journey to Somewhere

(or ramblings from a chaotic mind on mental illness, fear, anxiety, and depression—you know, the fun stuff)

by

Kimberly Anne Conway

DORRANCE
PUBLISHING CO
EST. 1920
PITTSBURGH, PENNSYLVANIA 15238

Dorrance Publishing Co
585 Alpha Drive
Pittsburgh, PA 15238
Visit our website at www.dorrancebookstore.com

ISBN: 979-8-89341-087-7
eISBN: 979-8-89341-586-5

In loving memory of
Dick Conway
Grandma Kelsey
Aunt Betty Jo

"There's nothing shameful about being afraid. It's… it's… I think it is
kind of brave to say you're afraid."
Whoopi Goldberg
The View
01.18.2024

Second Things First

Dear Reader,

I fully intended to have my first fiction novel written by the fall of 2023, or at least by the end of the year. While writing it, my lifelong companions, fear, anxiety, and depression kept fighting me every step. So I decided to embrace them more fully than ever before and put them on paper. Sigh… the results are this book which will be published way before the other one is finished.

The following is my journey—how it started, where I've been, and well, we don't really know how things end up, do we?

One thing I can say for certain is I have learned a lot about myself and most of it is good—a far cry from where I started. My hope is that if you see yourself in these pages, it gives you hope and comfort. If you don't see yourself, I hope you have empathy for those who follow a similar path to mine.

I didn't do this journey by myself, I had some actual real live companions with me and I would like to thank them. First I want to thank my Higher Power for putting people in my life when I needed them most and providing the answers I needed to continue forward—many times I got answers I didn't know I needed. Thank you to Terri for being my rock and cheerleader throughout this journey. Thank you to my therapist Leanne for helping me work through my questions and findings. Thank you to Shelley for agreeing to be my accountability coach and her patience as we navigated unfamiliar grounds. Thank you to my parents, Carole and Bart, daughter Emily and granddaughter Hazel for inspiration and hope. Thank you to Tank and Hershey who provide endless comfort, cuddles, and purrs. And to those who have been in my life forever, the Crazy Eight: Bonnie, Cindy, Leanne (not my therapist), Lisa, Stephanie, Teresa and Twila. Thank you for your friendship and encouragement.

This book is dedicated to those of us struggling with mental illness and those who love us.

Let the journey begin…

TABLE OF CONTENTS

1. Start writing a book.

2. Start writing a second book.

3. Have self-doubts.

4. Anxiety attack.

5. Go back to bed and never talk about it again.

Humble beginnings.

Innocence lost. A voice not heard.
An untimely death.

The unwanted travel companions of life.
It sucks.

And reality has many sides.

There's a special place in hell for some people.

Are you still with me?

Sometimes our part is we have NO part.

Where I am

1. Start writing a book.
2. Start writing a second book.
3. Have self-doubts.
4. Anxiety attack.
5. Go back to bed and never talk about it again.

As long as I can remember, I loved to write. I would spend hours under a tree in the front yard, writing until the sun went down. I would write long rambling poems about "Who am I?" "What is my purpose?" "Do I belong?" All the light-hearted things a young girl should think about.

So here I am. Sitting in front of a computer on a Sunday morning with millions of words and thoughts racing through my mind. It always amazes me when people don't know what I am talking about. I thought everyone had stories, characters, and words as companions in life.

Huh, weird.

Of course, my other daily companions are fear, anxiety, self-doubt, depression, worthlessness—all the fun stuff!

No longer a young girl, and in my sixties—it's never too late—I am going to put to paper some of those ramblings. Maybe they will help someone? Who knows? Either way, buckle up... here we go...

Growing Up Conway

Humble beginnings.

My mom and dad were teenagers when they got married. I was the only child for two years and then the other three came within the next three years. It was the early 1960s — rotary phones, three channels on a black and white TV — a simpler time.

And I want to make absolutely clear, I will never put any blame on my parents for the way I was raised or who they were. It's ALWAYS easy to look back and say coulda, woulda, shoulda, but that's not reality. We all have done the best we can with the cards we were dealt. Doesn't mean it was easy. It's not an excuse. It's life.

We lived in the country, very close to the Wisconsin/Illinois border. I remember spending a lot of time climbing trees and playing outside. Rainy days were spent playing board games or reading. Sometimes, I would crack open a cookbook and bake something.

Our house was small, six people, one bathroom (no shower) and all three of us girls sharing a room. My brother had his own room.

But I had a tree.

It was a special place that would be lovingly called "Kim's Tree" and kept that name long after we became adults. I was the only one who was able to climb it, and it became my own sanctuary. I think I spent more time by myself than with my siblings and the tree was "mine." Being the oldest and the others so close in age, most of the attention went to them. Looking back, I know I was loved, but I don't think I felt it too much.

Somewhere along the way, I felt my family was better off without me and that I was just in the way. I remember feeling surprised they even remembered my birthday. I moved to my grandma's house when I graduated high school and attended a nearby college. I believed my family would be better off if I wasn't there. Looking back, I missed so many things! I missed my siblings' games, concerts, and plays, but I didn't think it would matter if I was there or not.

Reading this will break my mom's heart and that is not my intention at all. She was a teenager, catapulted into an adult world, doing the best she could. She was number four of six kids and lived on a farm that also had an airport. The kids were left to run the farm while the parents were off in the bars or flying. It's interesting and sad, to hear of how she was raised. The grandma I knew and loved was not the same woman who raised my mom. I never met my grandpa, he died in a plane crash when she was sixteen. I think with the way she was raised and her young age, she did pretty darn good at raising us. And I don't know how she handled four kids within five years of each other!

My dad took any job he could to support us. He showed up at General Motors in Janesville (a forty-minute drive one way) every day looking for a job and every day they said they weren't hiring. His persistence paid off and he was finally hired. He always pressed upon us the importance of having a good job and wanted his children to be financially stable. During change-over or layoffs at GM, my dad worked at the locker plant in our small town. It was the local butcher store where farmers took their animals. I remember him bringing home hard rolls and a variety of lunch meats and cheeses for Saturday lunch. It was a welcomed treat.

My dad wasn't a fan of going to college. As a teenager he worked at a college in the city where he grew up. He lost his job when they found out his girlfriend was pregnant. It didn't matter they were going to get married and it tainted his view of higher education. I remember him saying the only reason I wanted to go to college was to smoke pot. Of course that wasn't true and I didn't have to go to college to smoke pot! My mom worked as a secretary after she graduated from high school, but lost her job when they learned she was pregnant. I understand it was a different time, but the last thing they needed was to lose their jobs.

My parents instilled in us a good work ethic, integrity, and honesty. They both worked hard. My mom worked several different jobs, including driving a school bus, a real estate agent, and eventually retired from the United States Postal Service.

My dad loved his job at GM, but was forced to take a disability retirement after an off-the-clock heart attack. He fought against it, he didn't want to retire. Unfortunately the Conway family has a long history of heart issues so the forced retirement was valid. His father died of a massive heart attack at the age of forty-three playing golf and left behind a wife and four teenage boys. My dad was the youngest at thirteen. It was a dark time for his family.

My dad was sure he was going to "die of the big one" too, but his story was a little different. He died at fifty-three of congestive heart failure a few years after retirement. He was given five years to live, but died eight months after he was diagnosed. The only solace in his death was he died peacefully in his sleep, during duck hunting on the Mississippi River. Despite his diagnosis, it was a bit of a shock. There is no cure for congestive heart failure, but he was doing so much better. He was on his longest streak of no emergency hospital visits. We had felt hopeful. I was thirty-five.

Okay, back to my childhood. Besides climbing my tree, I also spent days playing in the barn, looking for kittens, riding horses, and of course, writing. I'm going to probably use the phrase "looking back" many times. As I write this, I can see why I did some of the things I did. For example, any gray kitten found was mine. Calicos, tabbies of all colors, were common cats. Grays were not, so I "claimed" any grays. It was something out of the ordinary that made me feel special. Horseback riding also made me feel special. I was the only one of us kids interested in horses. My mom had a horse I could ride and I was lucky enough to have neighbors who let me ride theirs—if I could catch them on my own!

When my siblings got older, we would sometimes play games together. We had a version of tag we called spies. Basically, we just ran around in the dark trying to find each other and hide from each other at the same time. Our teams were usually the oldest and youngest against the two middles.

We lived on one of those farms where there was a big house and a little house. Our family lived in the small house.

We had an acre of land and chickens, ducks, rabbits, a horse, cow, and pet pigs. One pig, Corky, was fun-loving and as playful as any dog. The other, Petunia, was a nasty little snort. I remember her having my poor brother trapped on his toy tractor screaming, as she tried to bite him.

Our neighbors started as dairy farmers and I remember when the cows were brought across the road to the barn for milking. I can still smell the milkhouse and remember how we helped feed the calves. Of course, I'm not sure how much we actually "helped" as kids, but our neighbors never made us feel unwelcome.

Later, when our neighbors transitioned from dairy to pork, I would spend many hours playing with the pigs. I LOVED playing with the pigs. They were silly and fun and just adorable.

All in all, it was a wonderful place to grow up. There was a lane behind the house, leading to a small woods and a wooded pasture across the road. Imaginations were allowed to flow freely as many treasures were found exploring. I loved collecting rocks too.

Speaking of treasures and neighbors, I would proudly display my rocks, and charge my neighbors ten cents (not sure, maybe a penny) to come and see them. And if they were lucky, I would have written a play for my siblings to perform too.

Our neighbors were family. And as I would later learn, we were actually distantly related. We referred to the elders as Mr. and Mrs. As the story goes, I called them both Mr. Sommers. My mom explained that the man was "mister" and the lady was "misses." Always the rule follower, I started calling them Mr. and Mrs. And it never changed.

We had wonderful cousins, aunts, and uncles. My dad's mom, Grandmother Conway, moved to Montana. She was a teacher in Helena, Montana and her father, Great-Granddad Robinson also lived in Montana.

He claimed to be the first non-Native born there. He was the only grandfather I knew. My mom's mom, Grandma Kelsey, lived on the farm until the day she died. The farm is no longer there, but the memories remain.

Our family circumstances lay the foundation for who we are and family dynamics can be tricky. Being a parent is unchartered territory. My mom didn't have good role models to look to for guidance. We know what we know. Parents don't want their children to repeat their mistakes. And children don't always want to listen.

We all strive to be better, do better, and many times fall short. It's not because we *can't*, it's because we don't know *how*. Sometimes we work on trying to change. Although sometimes things change us. Things we have no control over. Things that will alter us, rewire us, and take us down paths no one should go.

These Three Things

Innocence lost. A voice not heard.
An untimely death.

~~~~~~~~~~~~~~~~~~~~~~

We were in the corn crib. He grabbed my hand and put it down his pants. I can still feel the coarseness of his pubic hairs and it still makes me shudder.

I was six years old.

I can't recall how many times it happened. And in trying to protect other innocents, I will not reveal any other information. He was a hired hand and one day he was gone. Someone must have seen something.

A year later I blurted something out at my grandma's house. My poor mom had no idea.

~~~~~~~~~~~~~~~~~~~~~~

Two of my uncles always had motorcycles and during a family gathering at our house, my dad thought he would try riding one around the block. (A block in the country is a LOT bigger than a block in a city.) The way our house was situated and only farmland to the east, we could see someone driving on the side road to go around the block. So being a concerned daughter, I watched my dad ride the motorcycle down the road. I never saw him turn on the side road. Nor did he continue down to the main road. I tried and tried to get the other adults to listen. Something was wrong! Dad never turned down the road! No one listened. Eventually, they became concerned when he didn't return and went out to look for him. Where should they start the search?

I knew where he was—why weren't they listening?!

Sure enough, he missed the turn and landed in the ditch. That is where he was found. He didn't have any life-threatening injuries, but did have a career-ending one—he was playing semi-pro football for the Delavan Red Devils at the time.

He hated motorcycles until the day he died.

~~~~~~~~~~~~~~~~~~~

Living in the country, there were not many children nearby. So when a neighbor boy, Eddie, was old enough, he would ride his bike to our house. We enjoyed having another playmate because going to his house wasn't always an option. They had German shepherds and they were perfect for protection, but not for visiting.

I remember my mom having a talk with Eddie about riding his bike home. She told him he needed to be careful when he got to his driveway. He didn't always look before crossing the road.

To this day, I can clearly see what happened—or didn't happen. I walked him down to the end of our driveway and reminded him to look before he crossed the road. I stood there and watched until he made it to his driveway. Sighing with relief, I turned away. I heard the crash and looked to see nothing but dust. Eddie had been hit.

And I didn't see the car either.

I ran to my mom and told her Eddie had been hit by a car. There was no such thing as 911 in those days. I remember being frantic. It just seemed like it took an eternity for her to understand what I was saying and get help.

He later died.

He was nine years old. I was eleven.
~~~~~~~~~~~~~~~~~~~

~~~~~~~~~~~~~~~~~~~~

Three traumatic events that happened between the ages of six and eleven. Decades later, we learned how traumatic childhood events can rewire our brains. Perhaps because of those things, I became a defender of others, all the while, believing I was not worthy of defending.

And at the same time, believed my voice didn't matter.

Right now, as I look back on this with tears running down my face, this is the place in time... this is the place in time where I began to believe that not only did my voice not matter, but neither did I.

I grieve for that little girl who felt so unwanted and unloved. Although it wasn't true, that is how she felt. That was her reality. That was my reality. I was just a child.

And I felt broken.
~~~~~~~~~~~~~~~~~~~~

Fear, Anxiety, Depression

The unwanted travel companions of life.
It sucks.

Ah yes, this is where my fellow travelers joined me in life. It was bad enough what happened at the tender age of six, but the other two incidents just seem to make things worse.

I never felt I mattered.

It wasn't until decades later that I learned how fear, anxiety, and depression impacted every aspect of my life.

In school, I always felt stupid. When I applied myself to a subject—something I found interesting—I usually did very well. Looking back, I think I was bored, school was boring.

However, in some odd way, school was my sanctuary. I never wanted to go home. I signed up for clubs and activities, anything to keep me occupied. I think I was longing to find a place to fit in, a place I mattered.

Looking back, I can see this is where I developed a pattern. I was good at a few things. And once I achieved something, I stopped. I quit.

I was one of the first two freshmen to ever make the pompon squad. It was quite the accomplishment! At first, it was exciting, but then self-doubt started creeping in. I began feeling I wasn't as good as the others and afraid I wouldn't remember the routines. I started skipping practices and eventually, was off the squad.

The pattern would be repeated throughout high school in different ways. I remember one time during a tennis match I was soundly defeating my opponent in the first set. She said to me, "I can't believe you are a number six," referring to my place on the team. I completely fell apart the rest of the match. I felt bad for beating her. I was as high as number four at one time on the team. Whenever someone challenged me for my spot, I just couldn't pull out the win. I didn't have the mindset or the self-confidence to succeed.

I did enjoy playing doubles. I was good at the net and in my senior year, I had a great partner who was good at the baseline. We were the number two team on the squad and getting better each match. We were looking forward to tournament time. And then I blew it. I was at a wedding reception and was drinking. I was suspended for an athletic code violation and not able to participate for two weeks—the two weeks of the tournament. I felt so bad for my doubles partner.

The only regret I had was not addressing the situation better. The other athletes only had to miss two games, whereas I missed more, due to the amount scheduled during the suspension. I don't know if challenging it would have worked then, however, sticking up for myself was never a strong point. I was guilty. When asked if I was drinking, I was one of only a handful of students who admitted it. The ones who lied suffered no consequences.

If I had to do it all over again, I would still admit it. I would not have been able to live with such a big lie.

I made the varsity basketball team as a sophomore. And thank God for Cindy and Carol. I never felt I belonged or felt part of the team. It didn't help that Carol and I had to trade off practicing with a senior. She never wanted to come out. Coach would yell at us to get in there, but what were we to do? If he didn't tell us to switch, she wouldn't. We had fifteen on the team, and when the tournament came around, the roster had to be cut to twelve. Cindy, Carol, and I were cut. Coach said he made the choice because I was a sophomore. And then went on to say, "Even if you are better than a senior."

We still went to practice and still supported the team a thousand percent. It hurt though. And I felt more than ever, I didn't belong on the team.

Our junior year, Cindy asked to be moved to the junior varsity team where she could get a lot more playing time. I asked the coach if I could go too, but he said he needed me as a back up to one of the senior starters. But I wasn't used that way, I felt he had no faith in me. The good thing that happened was I practiced a lot against the senior starter and she was a phenomenal player. Practicing against her didn't give me the playing time I needed to boost my confidence, however, it did help build my rebounding skills and that was one thing I did very well.

By my senior year I was a some-time starter. My mom would say I always did great when I came off the bench, but struggled when I started. Looking back, I think it was the same old pattern. I worked my butt off to get there and when I got there, didn't think I belonged there. I remember one game I started and came out strong. I had a couple of steals right off the bat and was just out there playing, there was no self-doubt, no anxiety. It was like freedom—I was focused and in the zone. Halfway through the first quarter the coach pulled me out. I was surprised. He only pulled us out if we were screwing things up. He looked at me and said, "I thought you needed a break." What I internalized was *you were doing great, but you need to stop. You cannot be great.* The feelings came tumbling down, I'm not supposed to be good. I sure was carrying a lot of baggage around.

We were a senior heavy team, with three juniors and twelve seniors. Once again when tournament time came around, three had to be cut. This time it was three seniors. I remember I went to them and said I was sorry this happened. I just wanted to offer some comfort. I wasn't a captain; I was just trying to be the teammate I didn't have as a sophomore. One of them wasn't having it and ripped into me. Despite the negative response, I realize now it is something positive I carried forward in my life. When a situation arose that didn't directly affect me, but I had the ability to help, I would ask myself "What kind of supervisor, coach, friend, co-worker or employee would I need right now to make things a little better?" I tried to be the cheerleader, support system—and as a former co-worker once said—the mother hen who gathers everyone under her wing. Huh. I never knew where that came from and now I know.

The one sport I felt I excelled at was track and field. I held the shot-put record for nine years and was captain and MVP my senior year.

I felt different in track. It was the only time in school—in all my activities—I had confidence and I don't know why. I ran the 220 (now the 200), 880 (800) relay, shot and discus. Sometimes I was put in other events. I practiced the high and long jumps, but never did those in a meet. I ran the 110 (100-yard dash) and 440 (400) relay. Every year—freshman through senior—I held a school record, be it individual or relay team.

Coach Baxter knew just how to push me, and I trusted him completely. One meet he came to me and said, "I need you to run the 220 hurdles."

I looked at him stunned and said, "I haven't even practiced the hurdles."

He was dead serious when he replied, "It's just like the 220 except you have to jump every once in a while."

Okay, I went and did it. I was doing great until the last three hurdles. I nicked the third from last, completely knocked down the next one and barely made it over the last one. But I finished!

Another favorite story is when he needed me to run in the mile relay. Now I never ran—other than a leisurely jog during warmup—a full lap around the track. Oh boy, here we go. I was the third runner. The first two runners got us a comfortable lead. I was halfway around the track when I heard him yell "They're catching up to you!" I gave it all I could and passed off the baton. I looked around. The other runners were not close at all.

I still smile when I think of track. As I mentioned earlier, I don't know why it felt different. And I don't think I really recognized it at the time. Maybe it was because Coach challenged me in practice and at meets. Or was it I felt he had faith in me?

During particularly hard workouts, he would say, "You'll pass out before you die." It became our mantra.

We didn't have, as far as I know, organized sports for girls until my freshman year of high school. And if I am correct, that means I am the first girl to letter in track all four years. I wasn't a superstar, however I was a consistent performer. I never made it out of regionals or was a conference champion, although in shot-put, I was undefeated in conference meets my senior year. I lost by less than an inch at the All-Conference meet and finished second. My last regional meet I broke my own school record.

Tennis and track were both individual endeavors, but the confidence level was completely different. And basketball was the sport I loved the most and yet mentally, I struggled. I know now, I learn better by doing than by lecture or following drawn-out plays. I need to physically run through the play and not just see it on paper or a chalkboard. I am able to do it if given enough time to visualize it. However, if I am under stress or experiencing anxiety, I am not going to grasp it at all. Maybe that is where the struggle started. I felt stupid I couldn't grasp things as fast as others. But once I had them, they were locked in.

Sometimes, I wish I could go back in time and play basketball my senior year again. With the knowledge I have now of course!

And somewhere along the way, in all the chaos, I found the best friends ever. I asked them one day, how did we become friends? It was an interesting conversation. We were always in and out of each other's lives—girl scouts, church, 4-H, band, sports, and school. Five of us started kindergarten together. Cindy came to our school in third grade. We became friends when I showed her to the bathroom. Later, her family joined the church my family attended. We just evolved. By the time we hit high school, we were thick as thieves.

There were other people we hung out with too through the years and cherish their friendships, but there was something about the eight of us, the Crazy Eight.

We still get together, and thanks to technology, have monthly or bi-monthly computer chats. We've gone through weddings, divorces, births, deaths, our darkest hours, and joyful times. We enjoy escape rooms (Leanne rocked that last one!) and just hanging out. I don't know how I would have made it through school—let alone life—without these ladies by my side.

Love always to Bonnie, Cindy, Leanne, Lisa, Stephanie, Teresa and Twila.

Perception Is Reality

And reality has many sides.

I want to pivot a little here and emphasize I am not putting any blame on anyone—at this point anyway. My parents never had any intention on making me feel like I didn't matter. In fact, I will need to talk with my mom before this book is published. I don't want to hurt her. We all can look back on our lives and wished we could have done things better or differently. We can't. We did the best we could with the knowledge and tools we had at the time.

The only thing my parents "did" to me, was be parents. Both of their homes were upturned by death. Where my dad had some semblance of structure at home, my mom did not. They married as teenagers and did the best they could with the knowledge they had and their limited life experiences.

Every generation has had something deemed normal that would not be acceptable today. Punishments were more severe and secrets were rampant. Family issues stayed in the homes and did not go to the courts. Years later, we would learn about the horrid living conditions some of our classmates went home to. Then we would understand why they acted the way they did in school. I remember a friend telling me how she hated God for a long time. She would go to church and hear how God loved her as her family did. Then she would go home and see how her father abused her mother and how the oldest brother molested all his siblings. So much for God's love.

Compared to some of my classmates, my family life was normal. Yes we were spanked, perhaps on occasion a little harsh, but that was the way it was. My parents were strict as far as curfews were concerned and I think I spent most of my senior year grounded.

As normal as it was, it didn't stop me from feeling I was less than. That was my reality and no one had a clue what I was feeling.

My dad was my first coach. I remember him working with me on punting, passing and kicking a football. The goal was to enter me in the Punt, Pass and Kick competition that started in 1961 the year I was born. In the end, I didn't compete. I'm not sure why I didn't, but I think it was because I was scared. I would be the first and only girl to do it. Could it be this is where my starting and not finishing began? Could this be where I thought, okay I proved I can do it, why go any further? Or was the message no matter how hard I worked, I would not be any good. I wasn't perfect. I wasn't good enough. All of these thoughts just occurred to me as I was editing this chapter. It's interesting—to me anyway.

Fast forward a few years to junior high school and my dad would have open gyms for my female classmates and me to play basketball. There were no organized sports for girls at that time and luckily the principal of the school went to our church. Getting the keys was easy.

And finally he was my coach for summer softball and it was rough. I could do nothing right in his mind. He told my mom (who was also on the team) he had to be hard on me because I was his daughter. The team's sponsor at the time had a daughter that tried out and did not make the team, but I did. Could that be the reason he was so adamant about not showing favoritism? I remember one practice my dad was particularly hard on me. One of my adult teammates asked my dad, "Why don't you yell at us? Kim's not doing anything wrong!" Was this when the message of no matter how hard I tried, I would never be good enough, was fully embedded in my soul? My basketball coach was a yeller. Did I relate his coaching style to my dad? My track coach was not a yeller. He was supportive and positive. Is that why I reacted differently in each sport? I don't even want to try to figure out tennis. Then again, the answer might just pop up somewhere else in this book.

Fast forward one more time to my adult years. I was still playing summer softball and had made the All-Star Team. I invited my parents to come and watch me. And I sucked big time. I was so embarrassed. Not too long ago I brought that game up to my mom. She said it was just like when I started in basketball vs coming off the bench. I thought that was an interesting perspective. I wonder how to change that? Sometimes I don't even know what is happening until it's over. So how can I recognize this? And what exactly is this? I'll talk with my therapist about this and let you know.

So back to perception is reality. People grow up in the same family, experience the same things and yet have different realities. I didn't remember any of my siblings being down at the end of the driveway when the neighbor boy left that day. My mom said we all were (except her). I told my brother I don't even remember seeing the car go by our house. He said he did. He would have been seven. I wonder how it affected him? I didn't think to ask him and he might not even know.

How does being the oldest, middle or youngest child affect a person? If one person gets picked on more than another, does that make them become more stubborn in their views later on in life? Were they tired of people not taking them seriously so they make their point and stick to it no matter what? Did the younger children see the older one get in trouble and silently vow to always follow the rules? If they saw their oldest sibling fight to be heard, did they decide to keep things inside?

Perception and reality. Sometimes it's a delicate balance and sometimes a greater puzzle than we could ever imagine.

We're not prepared for life and may not even know we have picked up hitchhikers along the way called depression, anxiety, and fear. People don't react the same to situations and not everyone is motivated the same way. There is no flow chart we can follow that will lead us to figure out each step of life or try to help someone else maneuver through the maze. We also don't recognize how situations and emotions can be so entangled and affect so many aspects of our lives.

I think things may be a little better for people today—at least for mental health. The stigma of mental illness has lessened and counseling—better counseling—is more readily available. Asking for help is a sign of strength.

Now on to some harder stuff.

The Hardest Chapter to Write

There's a special place in hell for some people.

I have an uncle who was a pilot. He spent many years living in the United Arab Emirates. Whenever he came home, it was full of family gatherings. It felt like he was celebrated, put on a pedestal for all to admire.

On one such occasion I was living at my grandma's house and it's also where he stayed when he came home. He took me to dinner and bought me my first martini—how lucky I was to be his niece!

Until he came to my room one night.

I was eighteen or nineteen, don't remember for certain, but I do remember what happened. He started talking and then kissed me and started fondling me. I froze. I didn't know what to do. My grandma's bedroom was below me and my other uncle was down the hall. What was happening? What should I do? I can't fight back—can I?

My mind was racing. Fear was running through my body. Someone help me, I silently screamed. And then the most ridiculous thought came through my mind. "Tell me you love me," I said to my perpetrator. Somewhere my being was trying to rationalize something so horrific. Tell me you love me? How sick and disgusting was that? That's all I had? Yeah, that's all I had. You didn't have sex unless you loved the person. I learned that in church. So, if he loved me, that would make it okay, right? Right?!

He went down on me, and I was totally disgusted, appalled, humiliated, and scared.

And my body betrayed me.

I hated myself. I hated myself more than I could ever had imagined. I was a worthless piece of crap. And I was mortified.

The next night before I went to bed, I grabbed a steak knife and put it under my pillow. If he came to my room again I was ready. I heard him coming up the stairs and pressed myself tightly in the fetal position, facing the wall. He walked to my bed whispering my name. I did not roll over. He shook my shoulder. I did not roll over. My fingers were curled around the steak knife. I wasn't going to use it, I didn't think so anyway. I wasn't able to protect myself the night before, so what made me think tonight would be different? But it felt good to have it there. He left my room. I succeeded. I was able to protect myself. Shortly after, he returned to the UAE, however more importantly, he never came to my room again.

It took many decades to process what happened. I learned I was not the first, nor the last of his victims.

Things came out again about fourteen years ago. I think my sister had a conversation with his wife and things were brought to light. The wife wanted specifics, she wanted clarification: When exactly did this happen? Were they together at the time? He is a Christian now (gag me). My uncle wanted to talk with me and somehow, got my phone number. He called a couple times and left a voice message. I called my mom hysterically. I felt he was violating me all over again. I had nothing to say to him and definitely didn't want to hear from him. He had the audacity to tell my mom , he never did anything to anyone that they didn't WANT him to do.

No asshole. You never did anything to someone you didn't GROOM them to do.

I was young. I tried to find a way to survive what was happening to me. I tried to rationalize, find anything in my brain to quell the panic inside. And then on top of it all, my body responded, and I felt totally betrayed by it.

I have never stopped punishing my body for what happened. Although I was never skinny—my family genes are big butts and thighs— I was never fat. However, this is when I started putting on weight. I rationalized if I was heavy, no one would look at me. Fat was my safety net, my shield, and food was my comfort. I would learn years later that food can be addictive the same as alcohol and drugs. Food was also an acceptable addiction in my extended family who frowned upon alcohol.

This is the first time I totally, and completely, told someone every detail that happened. Congratulations world. Maybe I can finally heal and be at peace.

Oh, and yeah, I took his stereo when I moved out of my grandma's house. Her house was his landing spot when he returned to the States and he had a very nice stereo. He took my innocence; I took something from him. I felt he owed it to me.

Years later, his wife found out about the stereo and demanded $100 (they weren't even together at the time of the incident). I eventually paid the $100 just to put an end to it all. There is absolutely no reason to ever have contact with them again. Well, that was a fun chapter.

Checking In

Are you still with me?

How are you all doing? It doesn't get easier or light-hearted, so I thought we could use a little break right now. Take a big breath… hold it… slowly release…

Computers are an amazing invention; I highly recommend them. I can remember—I use those three words a LOT, don't I—typing papers on a typewriter. Liquid white-out, special "erasable" typing paper, it was a hard cruel world back then.

And spell check! Not sure I am 100% on board. At one time, I was a decent speller. Now I rely a bit too heavily on spell check. It took me several hours to remember how to spell audacity. I even cracked open the dictionary to find it. Nope, ad… od… adda… ugh… how do you spell it? And as all things happen, it popped in my mind at 5:30 this morning… au… it starts with AU!! Now keep in mind, I am NOT a morning person. But the word was so important, I got up and started writing. I had to put it in the book! Thank goodness for computers—easy fix. However, the computer did lack the intuition on what word I was actually looking for. Tsk. Tsk.

Hold on! As I sit here scolding my computer, I realize that is really risky business. Computers can also be fickle and make our lives miserable. Sorry computer—wait—would you like a name? Since you are also on this journey with me, a very important piece, part? Oh don't hate me! Nice computer… I love you…

I would like to take a moment to recognize my official unofficial editors, Lisa and Stephanie. Lisa and Stephanie, readers. Readers, Lisa and Stephanie. From the Crazy Eight, I asked them to be part of my journey too (not as important as you computer… you're so pretty). Of all my friends, Lisa and Steff have always been honest with me. Not that the others haven't, it's just they can be a little wishy-washy trying not to hurt feelings. If I was going to do this, I needed straight-forward honesty. And having this placed in only a couple of hands (well, I guess four) would be less chaotic than adding ten more. You have never experienced us trying to make a group decision. Sorry computer, I know you have during our many video chats, you brave soul. And on we go…

For the Survivors

Sometimes our part is we have NO part.

Unfortunately, sexual assault and abuse will never go away. I would like to think though, we are better at helping the lives that have been so cruelly harmed.

Victims/survivors blame themselves. We search for ways to deal, process and sometimes, just try to get out of bed. Some things we remember right away, others take years. We block them out, we try and rationalize. We go to therapy, we harm ourselves, or others. We bargain and plead to the universe. We get angry, cry, scream. While we are suffering and struggling, do you know what the perpetrators are doing? Nothing. Absolutely nothing.

They have little shame or guilt. Why should they? If anything, they are looking for the next "mark," the next person to groom. Sometimes, they find religion and hide behind that, all along either continuing or justifying their actions. And speaking of justifying, those who have knowledge of what is happening and ignore it, are just as disgusting.

When a friend of mine told her dad what her older brother had been doing to her all these years, his response was "Growing up, everyone did their sister in my neighborhood." Another friend was told by her mom, "Well you were very beautiful and matured quickly."

So many women and girls have been violated by male family members. Another friend struggles with being molested by her younger brother. She beats herself up over and over because she was the older sibling. Sexual perpetrators don't care about the dynamics. It's all about power and self-satisfaction. We are just something they use.

Abuse is not limited to female victims and male perpetrators. Many men and boys are victims too and females can also be perpetrators. In no way do I want to dismiss any victim of abuse. In the early 1980s I did a paper in college on males who were victims of domestic violence. There was very little information to be found at the time and there was no internet to search. As the years go by more males are coming out with their stories of abuse. When I was in junior high school, a teacher was quietly removed from teaching due to improper interactions with some of the boys. It was very hush hush. No one talked about it. I don't know who they were, but I have so much sympathy for them. Back in those days there was little if any counseling available. It makes me sick to think about what they went through and can't help but wonder how they are doing.

Schools, churches, heck even towns, will protect the perpetrators. We have seen it replayed over and over again in the news. I'm grateful it is reported; it's like shining a bright light on the fungus to kill it. Once the clouds of shame and horror fall, we can become the shining light. We are the ones that can make a difference. But it's so hard to do.

Everybody has a part in things that happen. And sometimes the part is we didn't have a part.

We didn't have a choice, so why would we have a part? Asking someone to tell you they love you before they rape you, isn't an invitation. It is survival. Fear triggers fight, flight, and freeze. Our beings don't have time to make a rational decision. We are in danger. We do things to survive. If we had any idea what was coming our way, we MIGHT be able to pick a different path.

We may hear the footsteps coming down the hall. We know what is going to happen. We may have the opportunity to hide or tuck ourselves against the wall with a steak knife under our pillow. We may freeze and take the violation because after all, who would believe us over the "chosen one." Or maybe we take it because we want to protect another sibling from the same abuse. To fight back isn't always an option, however it also is NOT an invitation. They came to us; we did not go to them. They had a plan.

Calculated moves. And they certainly didn't care about us or any consequences.

Sex is a natural bodily function. Some perpetrators justify response as validation we wanted it or they did nothing wrong because we "enjoyed" it. There is a false narrative that males cannot be raped if they are aroused. Just because we are steeped in fear, does not mean our bodies won't respond. As humiliating and disgusting as it is, we need to not hate our bodies. Someday I will get there.

There is hope and you are loved. It doesn't always feel like it, I understand, I sure do understand. It's a hard "club" to belong to, however, I hope there's some comfort in knowing you are not alone.

The Second Hardest Chapter to Write

ALWAYS listen to that inner voice.

Eight years ago I was hanging with some of my favorite people in the world, when something happened that took me down a rabbit hole I hadn't been in for a while. We were hanging out playing games and just enjoying each other. It had been a long time since we had been together. I was sitting at the table when one of my least favorite people came and sat next to me. Everything in my being screamed, "GET UP AND MOVE!" But I didn't. There was another voice rationalizing and telling me I was in a safe space and nothing was going to happen. He started rubbing my back while sitting next to me. The alarms were going off—MOVE!! MOVE!! But I didn't. What could possibly happen in front of all these people?

The next thing I know his hand was under my shirt and he said, "Women like having their skin rubbed under their bra." I was paralyzed. I don't remember what happened, but the next thing I knew, he was leaving and I was just sitting there stunned. The gathering seemed to end shortly after and when I went to my room, I had a complete breakdown.

I was violated. How did I let that happen? Why didn't I listen to the warnings? I didn't protect myself. Did anyone see what happened? How could I be so stupid? I thought I was safe. Never, ever, ever again assume you are safe—especially around him—and listen to those warnings!

It was a very long night. I called two people and had long conversations about what happened. He was no longer in the house and I knew I really was safe—this time—but still had a hard time sleeping.

It took me out of enjoying my favorite people. The gentle teasing and bantering that was fun the day before, was not fun the next day. It took on a life of its own and made me feel unloved and depressed. My poor favorite people had no idea what I was going through, they just knew something had changed. It had nothing to do with them and everything to do with what happened to me.

I was trying to fight through it, but I couldn't. What should have been a fun day was clouded by my mood.

It literally took me years to get out of the funk that surrounded me. I was triggered back to the time my uncle entered my room. I became paralyzed and then started berating myself for not protecting myself. This was a very dark time for me. I wanted to die, but I wasn't going to do it TO me, I was hoping for a car crash or something. I was so disappointed when I would wake up day after day still alive.

Between trying to work through that, the stress of my job and my daughter's upcoming wedding, I found myself in the emergency room with chest pains a few weeks later. I was struggling to breathe. They ran tests, but the results did not indicate a heart attack. I was admitted and more tests were run the next day. Everything looked good as far as my heart was concerned. That was a relief.

What I had experienced was a full-blown panic attack. I have experienced a couple more since that time, but none to that degree.

I have learned a lot these past few years about panic and anxiety attacks. Terri, my life partner, has been by my side these past eight years and can sometimes recognize my anxiety level is high before I do. And so does Hershey, one of my cats. When I am feeling particularly anxious, she will insist on sitting on my chest. It actually does give me comfort. I have also learned some techniques that have helped deescalate my anxiety: Big deep slow breaths. Rubbing my forehead and continuing down to my chin repeatedly. Shaking my hands side to side or up and down like I am waving very fast.

When things start to escalate my telltale sign is a certain sounding cough that sometimes leads to vomiting. It helps when I hear Terri yell out "Breathe!" After the episode is over she will gently ask, "What was that about?" Sometimes I know what caused it and sometimes I have to think about it. I used to try to ignore it and bury it—whatever "it" was at the time. I have become better at expressing what caused it and it helps that she is supportive—my safe place.

We had just started dating when this all happened. She didn't run away. She was one of the people I called that night and was very supportive and kind. Together we are learning how to navigate these unfamiliar waters. I am lucky to have her in my life.

And I will always listen to that inner voice.

2023

We interrupt this book to bring in a New Year.

Happy New Year. I chose to stay home this year. After many years of bringing in the New Year with friends, I chose to stay home. After wanting and longing for a person to be with, I chose to stay home. It was a strange decision for me to make, but one I felt I needed to make.

In all honesty, it was my anxiety that made the choice, or rather, put the thought in my head. Isolating is not always a good decision for someone struggling with mental illness. It is the one thing I do to perfection. I could stay home for days without contact with another human being. However in this case, it felt a little different. I want to make changes and I needed some "alone time" to prepare.

I want 2023 to be "my year."

I want to publish the other book I am writing, and hopefully, this one too. I want to quit my part time job and just do what I have wanted to do my whole life: Be an author. Publish a book.

And I need to put my life passengers—depression, anxiety, fear, self-loathing, and unworthiness—in the trunk of the vehicle. I want to stop letting them steer or be the back seat drivers. I want to, no need to, be the driver of my life. My Higher Power is the only other driver or co-pilot I want in my life.

It's hard. I spent the past four days trying to prepare for the New Year. I worked on my office and bedroom. Cleaned the kitchen, put away clothes—all "normal" chores that can bring me to my knees. I know it seems strange and I wish I could explain it. I am in my early sixties and should be able to keep a clean house. But sometimes it is so overwhelming. I know I mentioned it before that this is an issue I have been working on with my therapist. Just putting away laundry today gave me anxiety. I don't know why. I don't know why finishing something is so hard. I use my tablet—or the TV—as distractions. And then it is either too late or I am too tired to finish or start. Accomplishing a task, makes me feel lighter. Writing, makes me feel happy. A clean house, an uncluttered bedroom and office, gives me peace.

I recently bought a new bedroom set and removed the TV from my room. It has become a very comfortable and peaceful room. When my office becomes a dumping ground for empty boxes and other things, it disturbs the flow of the room. It's like something is clogged in my being. It makes it harder to write.

Of course, I like the other rooms clean too. There's something special about walking into a room that is tidy.

I look at my house and I am grateful for what I have. And then I feel guilty for what I have. Am I punishing myself? Am I being prideful?

Sometimes I think about those who are struggling to make ends meet and those living on the streets. Why them and not me? These thoughts weigh me down. Is this why I struggle with housework? Do I feel I don't deserve having a roof over my head? Do I feel I don't deserve to be happy? Sometimes. Sometimes I feel these things.

I have always felt more comfortable in failure than success. Why did that teenage girl struggle as a starter, but did good coming off the bench? I am a good leader and willing to help others succeed. I am everyone's biggest cheerleader—but not mine. Why? I don't understand.

Writing this second book has been a helpful tool as I write my first book. It has allowed me to examine why I do/did things. It has also brought me a lot of questions!

I did miss bringing in the New Year with my friends, and that first kiss of the year. I have a lot of anxiety going into 2023, but I also have hope. My office walls are filled with quotes, affirmations and encouragements. It also has positive energy, it feels good.

Here I am 2023. Let's do this.

Moving Forward While Looking Back

We can't ignore the past.

People will say things like "you need to move on," "the past is the past," "let it go"—none of which is constructive or helpful. In order to achieve this, there are things we need: Some understanding of what happened. The ability to process what happened and a good therapist... and possibly some medication.

I know therapy can be a scary thing for people. For me, it helps validate feelings, understand why I have those feelings and gives me tools to do things better.

I took a four-day break before starting to write this chapter, and I still went back and forth between the others. I did some editing trying to figure out what fits, what doesn't and how to make it flow. I didn't want to drag you through my whole life, just to get where I am right now. Because you see, I don't always understand why I do things now, until I look back and see/find the patterns.

So, what fits in this chapter and what fits in earlier? Ironically it gives me anxiety thinking about it. I remember the times I start things and never finish. It could be as simple as coloring a page in a book, I LOVE adult coloring books and all the pens and pencils that come with them. I feel like it helps unwind my brain, it relaxes me.

I beat myself up for not setting aside enough time to write and then I get stressed out even more. Some people may call it procrastination, but it is deeper than that. It is fear. It is anxiety. And it doesn't matter if it is sitting down and writing or laundry, dishes, gardening—anything. I see how much needs to get done and get overwhelmed. Sometimes, depending on the task, self-doubt trickles in too. Why even start? You know you can't do it perfectly, so why even try? My therapist helps me a lot with this—just start doing one thing. It could be folding one basket of clothes, doing the dishes—you know it really doesn't take that long to do dishes (putting away folded clothes is another story!). Sometimes I have to do that exact thing, just break it down and focus on one thing. And guess what? Many times, it turns into several things getting done—or several pages getting written.

One of the wonderful things about computers (I love you computer) is I can skip around as thoughts enter my mind and as I am trying to figure out how this all fits.

Usually when I start writing, things flow out, sometimes I sit and stare. That's when I stop focusing so hard and just start typing away—anything that comes into my mind. This is one of those times—lucky you.

I had a lot of dreams and one of them was being a sportswriter. I love high school sports of all kinds and enjoy following different teams from different schools. The Beloit Daily News had an opening for a sportswriter. I applied and got the job. I think I wrote two articles? Not sure. I remember covering football and volleyball—I couldn't wait until basketball season! But I failed, or rather my fear and anxiety took hold. I remember being at the BDN office writing my story. I think I must have been sighing a lot, because I noticed looks between the editor and another writer.

My fears of not being good enough, were raging through my mind. Both articles turned out rather well, due to heavy editing. I didn't understand completely, that was the job of an editor. I took it as failure. My words were not good enough. It wasn't until a couple years ago, I understood that was the job of an editor.

One of the sportswriters, Rob Lucas, wrote about how the editor, Jim Franz, made his stories even better. I always admired Rob's columns and was surprised his stories would have been edited, he is a really great writer.

Hmm maybe I wasn't a bad writer after all, Jim was just doing his job and made my stories better. Perhaps if I had stuck around longer, I would have realized it as things got easier. But I didn't. Those nasty life travelers brought me down. I had stopped asking for assignments. I felt defeated.

I didn't even pick up my last paycheck, I felt so unworthy.

Unworthiness, fear, anxiety, and depression are part of my past and present. Hopefully this journey will help me understand more about myself so I can lessen their impact on my future.

And it seems the further along I get in my writing, the more stuff comes out. The key *is* to let it go, however, I need to process it first. I think it is getting easier for me now that I am in a "safe" place. And by that I mean I am able to voice out loud my feelings without being told it isn't true. I am able to have time to understand why and/or how I reacted to something.

I remember arguments in past relationships about doing dishes and other chores. The expectation of having to do things exactly the same as the other person or it was wrong. I never understood the logic of that—and it was the core of the argument. As long as the chore got done and done correctly, what difference did it matter *how* it was done? And then afterwards came the "inspection" where every little thing was scrutinized to ensure it was done properly. I wasn't a child. I was an adult in a supposedly adult relationship, yet treated as a child. It became harder and harder to want to do anything around the house because not only was the threshold of perfection high, so was the criticism over every little thing.

Maybe this is why simple chores can be a struggle and give me anxiety. I keep expecting to be scrutinized and criticized. Terri doesn't inspect my work. If I don't get something done, I let her know that I will get it done and that is that. And if I forget do to something—there is always that one pan somewhere I forgot. I will look at the stove and not see it until the dishes are done and poof! There it is! It is something we laugh about because we both do it. Happily, perfection is not part of our relationship.

This is why writing this book is good for me. Realizations about how the past is effecting my present. I am in a safe place where I don't have to worry about being criticized and expected to do things only one way. There are expectations and when they aren't met, we talk about it. I am treated as an equal not as a child. Whew… I can actually feel some of that crud releasing from my being. It feels good. It feels like peace.

Terri and I come from two different worlds. Her world uses a lot of swear words and mine does not. It has been an adjustment for me. A simple sentence from her with a swear word in it can make me shutdown. I only swear if I am really, really angry—and it takes a lot for that to happen. So even though it is really a minor thing, it has an effect on me. I relate swearing with anger. For her it is normal. She shouldn't have to tip-toe around me and be guarded about everything she says. It falls on me to figure it out and talk about it.

See how "easy" that was? I wanted to get something down before I went to bed and berated myself for not writing enough today. And walla! I wrote more than just a few minutes.

I also learned some things and processed some things. I feel more at peace than I did when I started. Thanks for being on this journey with me.

Morning Thoughts

Positive pieces and sourdough.

I'll let you in on a little secret. I have finished the chapters in this book and now I am going through to self-edit and expand on chapters that are not fully developed. There is one chapter towards the end I may delete, however, I did not expect I would be adding a new one. Surprise! Here it is!

My mind works all night long. I have very bizarre dreams and sometimes wake up with weird thoughts going through my head. One morning I woke with "What if strawberries had diapers?" in my head. Another day I had dreamt I wrote a Broadway play called "Pete Davidson the Musical" complete with a rap type song. I don't rap, but I was doing it in my dream!

This morning I woke up with gratitude. There were three men who had put positive energy in my life and showed me I was worthy. I didn't realize it at the time, but I did this morning.

Don Desing was the first one. I was friends with his daughter, Nancy, and together we had some fun escapades in high school—like the time we swore we would not take his T-bird on "the circuit" (a place in Janesville with one-way streets that teenagers from all over the county came on a Friday and/or Saturday night to hangout. Sometimes you would pull over to talk, but mainly it was just driving around and pretending to be cool). We took the T-bird to the circuit, got a lot of attention from the boys and got into a minor accident. Every time I hear the Beach Boys song "Fun, Fun, Fun" I think of Nancy and that night.

Back to Mr. Desing. After I graduated from high school I got a temporary full-time job at a shoe manufacturing plant. My job was to fill the orders that came in. Mr. Desing was an executive at the company and I ran into him one day as I was naively looking for a left-handed screwdriver. I was too trusting and gullible so I was the perfect target for a prank. He was surprised to see me in his building and didn't know I worked there. I told him I was hired just for the summer. He took me directly to my supervisor and told her I would be working there as long as I wanted. I was surprised—and so were those who sent me looking for a left-handed screwdriver!

Mr. Desing did not have to do that. He saw something in me that I didn't. Where I thought so little of myself, this man thought different of me. He didn't know my work ethic, but he knew *me*.

Something else was happening at that time too. There was an employee whose only reason for working there, was he was the star football player for the local college. I use the word working very loosely—the only thing I ever saw him do was stalk me in the warehouse and block my way. The only way I could get past him was by giving him a kiss. It never escalated further and one day he was gone. He didn't last long. I never told anyone what was happening, although I think my supervisor might have suspected something. And the fact I knew Mr. Desing probably had a part in the football player leaving too. Mr. Desing had cast a protective spell on me by talking to my supervisor. I was left alone to do my job.

Mr. Desing died a few years ago. I wish I could have told him how much his kindness meant.

The second man owned a McDonald's. Shortly after I started working there, a girls basketball team was formed. We would play against area McDonald's teams. One game whenever I passed the ball to someone, they would pass it right back to me. I asked my teammate why she wasn't shooting and she said, "We were told that only you were to shoot."

I think this man knew me from high school and had watched me play. Putting together the McDonald's teams was a way to help me build confidence. I never realized it until much later and he never talked about it. He reminded me of my track coach only more reserved. He had a quiet, positive energy and I felt like he was always trying to find a way to help me without me knowing. I can't explain it and I could be wrong, but that is my perspective and also why I am not using his name.

One job I really enjoyed doing at McDonald's was working the grill. They wanted to train me on taking orders too and many people thought it was a "step up," but I didn't care. I enjoyed the grill. Eventually I was scheduled to work during changeover—when breakfast switched to lunch. The older women running the front wanted me because I was good and I loved the challenge. The goal was to have very little left over from breakfast while turning up the grills and getting the lunch sandwiches done.

At that time, one of the "coveted" awards was The Golden Spatula given to those who excelled working the grill. I was given one. When I left that job, the owner pulled me aside and gave me another one. He didn't know if I had received one and wanted to ensure I knew I was appreciated. It was very appreciated.

The third person was of all people, a math professor (I had big time math anxiety that stemmed from a third grade teacher). I can't remember his name, but I will remember that is the first time someone actually told me I was smart. I felt I was struggling in his class and had just received a promotion at my part-time job. I would be working more hours and felt I needed to lighten my academic load. The math class I was taking was the obvious choice. The professor tried to talk me out of dropping. He told me I was smart and that I could do this. I was shocked. I was smart and could do math. Math?

I still dropped the class, but it was a turning point of sorts for me. I was smart. My high school guidance counselor tried to discourage me from going to college. He didn't believe I had the academic prowess to succeed. I went to college because that was what I felt I was supposed to do even though I didn't think I was smart—a thought validated by my guidance counselor. Finally after taking classes on and off for years, I did get my bachelor's degree graduating *magna cum laude*. Oddly hearing I was smart was one thing I actually accepted about myself.

Even though I had jobs before I graduated from high school, I do believe working at the shoe manufacturer and McDonald's gave me the confidence and work ethic I needed to be successful. And being told I was smart—and accepting that fact—was huge.

I can see—*and feel*—those qualities in my being. I can feel the foundation of who I am while digging out all the crap inside of me. Now I just need to work on accepting I am worth working for. I can give anyone else a thousand percent, but struggle doing the same for myself. But I have come a long way since I started writing this book.

And where does sourdough fit in? Well it's one of those rambling morning thoughts I found interesting.

This fall a wonderful neighbor asked if I was interested in some sourdough starter. I said sure, not having a clue what to do. At first I was very overwhelmed and thought there was no way I could do this process, it was too tedious and time consuming. I felt there was too much perfection required and that was just not me.

However, I continued to move forward. I found simple recipes, joined a sourdough starter group on Facebook and prepared to learn. I had a few mishaps, but usually was successful. My specialty is crackers. I make a variety of flavors and they are Terri's number one request.

But you know what I didn't do? I didn't start out like a crazy woman buying all the supplies and a Kitchen Aid mixer. In fact, I make everything by hand without a mixer. I only bought a few things like bowls that were easier to clean and a tool to make holes in the crackers. My daughter and son-in-law bought me a set of vintage ceramic bowls which I absolutely love!

All of this is different for me. I didn't want to jump in buying all the bells and whistles because I wasn't sure how long I would continue doing sourdough. And I see I don't need all the fancy things to continue. Whereas before I would hit the road running and then burn out, this time I eased in a little at a time and found it enjoyable. I may actually continue doing this for a long time!

This journey hasn't been easy, but I have learned a lot. I encourage everyone to try to put their past in words. You don't have to show it to anyone. Somedays when you are feeling things whirling around like a tornado inside, just write. It doesn't have to make sense. As I mentioned in the previous chapter, sometimes I stop thinking and just let the words flow out. In my case, some parts were useful and some didn't fit. The ones that didn't fit I put in a different document.

This is your book too. Mark it up, highlight it, make notes, add post-its—unless you borrowed it from the library then please don't!

Progress, not perfection, is what I strive for. And right now, right at this very moment, I am starting to feel a confidence awaken inside of me that has been sleeping for a long time. It's a calming sort of confidence—soothing in nature. I can feel encouragement to move forward without the anxiety and fear. Where are those pesky travelers at this moment? Maybe I have finally tied them up and put *them* in the trunk! However that pesky depression is still lurking around somewhere. I'm not going to look for it… just keep moving forward…

Social Media

To meme or not to meme?

There is a lot of talk about how social media affects teenagers and I am glad that it was not around when I was growing up. I didn't always make the best decisions and cannot imagine dealing with my mistakes blasted all over the internet. And as I stumble back down memory lane, the thoughts I had of being unworthy and not belonging would only have been magnified. I can understand why some parents are against their children being on social media. It is hard enough maneuvering life as a teenager without that added pressure.

Then I started thinking about the memes I see on Facebook that say you are responsible for your actions, feelings, how you deal with triggers, etc., etc. I want to tell people how hurtful that is to someone struggling. But if you aren't struggling or never experienced depression, anxiety, fear or triggers, you won't understand.

How would I know that one incident would trigger me into a depression and take me back down that rabbit hole? According to your meme, I'm responsible for it and I need to get over it and move on. According to your meme I need to stop dwelling on the past and move on. I can't fix it, move on. Leave your baggage behind and move on. If only it were that simple.

There are people who have had horrible things happen to them and they have moved on. There are others who struggle. No one person should determine how someone should deal with and get over their trauma, depression, and anxiety. We all have different genetic makeups and experiences. We all were raised differently too. I remember talking with a group of people about what my uncle did to me as a teenager. One of the men in the group was appalled I was eighteen or nineteen and *allowed* that to happen to me. Really? I thought I handled his insensitivity pretty well and did not take the bait he was dangling. He had had some trauma in his past, but instead of talking about it, it felt as if he needed to dismiss mine first so he could put his up on a pedestal. "Look at how bad *my* life was. This is what real abuse is about." He didn't actually say that, however that is what it felt like. Hey buddy, this isn't a contest I want to be in. There is no winner here.

As survivors we should offer support and not dismiss someone's experiences. He never got a chance to talk about his abuse because everyone was a little disgusted with his attitude. And I don't even really remember how any of it came up.

I was talking to someone recently who said, "When people say, 'just give them a hug and tell them you love them, they will get over it;' those people have no idea what depression is about." So true. If that is all it took to make it through depression, life would be very simple.

I was sharing with a friend of mine about this book I am writing and she shared with me similar feelings and experiences. We both talked about medications and therapy. And we both had a similar experience with a mutual acquaintance who would pooh-pooh us when we talked about taking a mental health day for ourselves. The acquaintance's response was always, "Big deal we all have issues. I get panic attacks once every one or two years and I have a pill to take." I'm happy that is all she needs to do and that is her experience. That is not mine nor many others.

It's hard enough to deal with judgement from people without being judged by people who walk a similar path. I will say it again, it is not a contest. There is no winner.

This is where I feel people on the outside looking in struggle. They see us hurting and struggling and don't understand why we just can't get over it. It's not that easy.

Mental illness runs through my mom's side of the family the same as heart issues run through my dad's. I think it's an interesting comparison although mental illness is a little more unpredictable. Mental illness is composed of many things, including trauma. Seeing a neighbor boy hit by a car will have different effects on those who witnessed it. Sexual abuse will rewire our brains, some people cope with it better—but why and how? Why do some people appear stronger than others in similar situations?

It could also be biological. Some people need medication—real medication. I believe there is a place for herbal remedies, however there are instances where medication is the only answer.

There were times in my life where getting out of bed was the best I could do. Those were the days I was sad to wake up alive. It's hard to express to people how it feels. Yes, I have a lot to live for, but the pain inside can be too much. When people commit suicide they're sometimes called cowards. I call BS. Until you have been in the situation where the pain inside outweighs any joy, shut up. I didn't always feel that way until I experienced the pain myself. It's different. Physical pain can many times be seen, fixed, and the cause can be found. Depression is something dark and painful living deep in our souls. It's easy to hide to the outside world, however living with it is a struggle.

What can you do to help? Nothing and everything. It's crazy. Some days I need to be alone in my thoughts. Some days being alone is the worst thing. It's hard to express what I need when I'm not sure myself. It's depression and anxiety and fear. It's mental illness. I think most people experience mental illness in one form or another. It could be biological, situational or seasonal. It's there. Meds and therapy help, but does it ever go away? I don't know.

Some of the worst things you can say to a person with depression is "What you need to do is…" Stop. What you don't understand is everything you are saying has been running around in my mind. There is nothing new you can say to me. In fact all it does is bring me down more. If I were actually able to do *any* of those things, don't you think I would?

Another thing is if someone is talking about what is happening, just listen. Don't interject your feelings or offer advice. Just listen. We don't want to have a debate and we can't always explain what is happening or how we are feeling. It's okay to ask questions for clarification and understanding, but please don't be disappointed or upset if we are not able to answer. Sometimes we just need to talk and the answer will present itself, but not always. I know that makes it hard on our families and our loved ones. And it affects everyone differently. Sometimes I'm fighting like hell trying to get the steering wheel away from the depression, fear, and anxiety who are driving the car. Sometimes I'm in the fetal position in the trunk. And many times I'm staring in panic sitting in the backseat.

Patience and love is what we need. I personally needs hugs. Lots and lots of strong hugs. I learned that is my love language. For a long time I didn't want hugs or anyone even putting a hand on my shoulder or arm. Don't touch me. My family were not huggers so the majority of touch I had growing up was bad touch.

I was molested by dads when they took me home after I babysat their kids. Maybe that was a reason I signed up for so many activities and got a job as soon as I could. That way I would not be available to babysit anymore. Wow. That was a new thought…

Social media is here to stay and something we do need to be able to maneuver around. We can avoid some of it and the stuff we can't we need to take with a grain of salt. People who have not walked in our shoes have no idea of our struggles and reaching out to them can sometimes make things worse. I know, I've done it. I've tried to explain how a post can hurt someone who is struggling, but they don't get it. Trying to get them to understand and *hear* me, just brought up too many unwanted feelings. The way it made me feel was not worth the time. Some people like to stir the pot and I will admit I have done it on occasion. I don't want to be that person anymore. We have options to block, unfriend and unfollow people who trigger us. I use the word trigger because on some level memes can bring up many different feelings. But then again you're not responsible for my triggers because your post says so. Sigh, it can be a vicious cycle.

I'm sure there will be some criticism about this book and I'm ready for it. I am ready in the realm of I don't care. If people want to criticize, go for it. I believe it will say more about them than me. I will treat it like the memes, they have little understanding of what they are talking about.

Now this is where my brain is going "But what if there are professionals criticizing and saying you are irresponsible for writing what you did?" Ugh. Stop. Just stop. I'm not writing this in a professional capacity or as a professional. I'm writing this as a person who struggles with mental illness on a daily basis. I can't think about what *might* happen, that will take me down a rabbit hole full of fear, anxiety, and self-doubt.

Breathe. Just breathe. Whatever happens will happen. And whatever happens in the future cannot change what is happening now.

It's okay. You're okay. I'm okay. We're okay.

Success! Finally!

The best six months.

I learned about twelve-step programs in 2009 after attending open Alcoholic Anonymous meetings with a friend. Alcohol wasn't my drug of choice, but food was. I joined Overeaters Anonymous that year and cried through most of my first weeks of meetings. I had found my people! And as I do most things, I started out with a bang and jumped right into it—I bought all the books and went to the conventions.

Abstinence would be fleeting though. Everybody has something they could binge on and it's different. It's not like drugs or alcohol where you may *feel* you need it; you don't need it to live. You need food to live.

Every day you're faced with your addiction. But what *is* your addiction? Sweet? Salty? White flour? Sugar? Or is it environmental triggers? Anxiety? Fear? Boredom?

Food was my crutch and I have an unhealthy relationship with it. Nutrition was not something we learned growing up. Recently a high school friend disclosed how she would eat several Twinkies before playing basketball. I would sometimes eat French fries at the downtown restaurant. Most times I went to school without breakfast and continued that as an adult. I went to work without a lunch and might have a candy bar or something from the vending machine. Basically I did not eat the whole day until I got home. And then it was bingeing the rest of the night. No wonder I could not lose weight. I was starving my body and it was hanging on to everything I put in it.

I frequently used food as a distraction. If I was the hostess I concentrated on the food and made plenty of it. Being busy with the food kept me from interacting with people. I also hid behind humor; if I could get people eating and laughing they wouldn't see what a horrible person I was. Yep it's true. I was always surprised when people liked me. Inside I felt like a terrible mess unworthy of friendship, let alone love. I kept things light and superficial—I couldn't let anyone in too far.

I remember after a cousin's wedding my sister was telling me about the things she learned from family during the reception. I asked her how she found out about all these things and she looked at me confused and said, "I talked to them." Talked to them? Huh, what a concept. Talking to people was scary, no, letting people know me was scary.

The first time I worked the steps in OA, my biggest fear was I would find out I wasn't a bad person. How crazy is that?! I always played the entertainer, the host, so people would like me. There was no way they would like the real person living inside. I believed the person inside was bad. And as I'm writing this, I'm not sure what that means. Maybe it's because I didn't like who I was and I didn't think anyone else would. That feels right.

Okay. I just looked up the definition of bad and there are many: Poor quality, substandard, inferior, second-class. Undesirable, unpleasant or unwelcome. Poor moral virtue or unacceptable conduct. Evil, immoral, wicked, corrupt. The words in the first two sentences fit, the rest doesn't. I'm not evil or any of those words. However being a lesbian, I was judged as lacking moral virtue and unacceptable conduct. I felt I had to put on a different face to be acceptable to the world. Even the house I once lived in had no pictures of us together on the walls—we didn't want anyone to feel uncomfortable walking into the house. How messed up is that?

And to be clear, I didn't think I was bad because I was a lesbian. It was who I was and I couldn't change it. Boy this is getting confusing. Let's try this, I think there were/are two things going on inside which I am just realizing and I never separated them: First of all I felt the need to hide that I was a lesbian. I had lost people I thought were friends, promotions and even benched on my softball team because I was gay. Secondly, my depression, anxiety, and self-doubt led me to believe I was not worthy of knowing or being loved. I didn't love myself, so who would love me. Wow, wow, wow. That is something I had never took the time to actually think about. They are two separate things.

I worked hard to keep my sexual preference hidden and as these things do, it all came out. There will always be those people who like to make things difficult because I am gay. They liked to stir the pot. However I did have some wonderful friends that made things better. They teased and treated me like a "normal" person. After all, wasn't I? I will forever be grateful for those wonderful people—if you worked with me or played volleyball with me—you know who you are!

At an Overeaters Anonymous meeting I put it out there I was gay and guess what? No one cared. No. One. Cared. It was a turning point of sorts. People actually liked me for who I was—they liked *me*.

I continued to struggle with finding abstinence until the spring of 2012. It was like a light switched on! I ran my first 5K in four years and it felt great! I was making great strides with food addiction and even became a sponsor. Physically, mentally, and spiritually everything felt aligned. It was a rare occurrence. Usually I could get one or two things in my life going well, but rarely three! By fall I was asked to speak on Steps 1-3 at a small conference. I was happy and feeling great…

Hold on now. You can't be happy and feeling great. STOP. Sigh… I don't understand why I do this. It's self-sabotage. I don't feel worthy of being happy. Yeah, I don't understand it either.

Sometimes I think a small part has to do with religion. We went to church every Sunday and it was usually boring. It took a while before I understood the difference between religion and spirituality. The ministers I connected with were spiritual, the other ones were religious. The spiritual ones you could see—and feel—the love inside of them. Religion can mess up your thinking too.

Step three talks about deciding to turn your life over to God or a Higher Power. I thought it would be the easiest step, after all, I was a Christian and had a relationship with God. Nope. Not even close. Through OA I learned it was okay to pray for help for myself. Hold the phone! It was okay to pray for *yourself* and ask for help and not just guidance? Somewhere along the way I believed it was selfish to do that. I mean, it was okay to ask God questions like, why am I here, what is my purpose, why does liver and onions smell so good but taste so bad? However, to ask for help was something different. It was selfish.

How many times have I told myself that I didn't matter? My needs didn't matter? Taking care of myself didn't matter? Everything was supposed to be about God and what He wanted us to do for **others** not ourselves.

And the flip side was the judgement. And one cannot be a Christian AND a lesbian. You have to pick a side. But God made me this way. Maybe, but you have a choice to not live in sin. Who said it's a sin? On and on and on…

And why do I have the right to be happy? People are hungry and homeless. Children are being abused. I don't deserve to be happy. I am not worthy of being happy. I spiraled down that rabbit hole with self-sabotaging thoughts as depression slowly slithered into the driver's seat and loosened my grip. I climbed in the backseat and started comforting myself with food. Yeah, so anyway, I had a solid six months of success.

The Knot

Untying the past to understand the future.

I am trying not to repeat myself, however, I am starting to see how intertwined things can become. I am trying to understand what I've done, why I've done it, and how to change it. It's all like one of those knots you get in the chain of a necklace. It's tight and you have no idea how it happened.

I learned a few things recently while talking with my therapist. Remember I said I would talk with her and get back to you. Perception is reality and my reality goes to the negative. I see my mom do this too. We go right to the worst of a situation and internalize things as our fault or jump to the worst scenario.

I told my mom she probably won't want to read this book and she agreed. I tried my best to explain how I felt that she and dad did the best they could in raising us and that it's always easy to look back and say we could do things better. It's true we can now, but not at that time. There are things with my daughter I wish I could have done better. The list could go on and on. I can only learn and try to do better now.

I am grateful my mom and I are getting closer. Our relationship has progressed so much lately. She has been telling me things about her childhood that break my heart and give me a better understanding of her. We are not that different. Both of us felt unwanted in our families, like we didn't matter. Her parents weren't present, however, mine were. I can see the similarities between the two of us. One thing I find interesting is when we are doing something, we need to focus on it completely and do not like interruptions. I don't recall seeing that in her while I was growing up.

I believe at two years old is when I first felt I was inferior, unwanted, and didn't matter. Within the next three years my siblings were born, and they required a lot of attention. I didn't understand any of it. I remember one time I climbed a different tree that I couldn't get out of when I was around five years old. I cried and cried for my mom to come and get me. She did and then told me not to climb it again. Of course, I climbed it again the next day. I remember struggling with the thought of asking for help or figuring it out myself. On one hand, I got my mom's attention and she had to take care of me. On the other hand, I got myself in a jam and probably should figure it out. I figured it out and got out of the tree myself.

One time I was barely five years old and my aunt took me to church. There were no other cars in the parking lot, but I assured her there was Sunday school and she dropped me off. I walked in and the minister told me there was no Sunday school that day. I made a mistake and corrected it by walking home—we lived three miles from town out in the country. A neighbor girl saw me walking along the road and took me home. My aunt was horrified (my mom was in the hospital after giving birth to my youngest sibling). When my mom found out she was very upset with the minister. He did not take the time to find out if I had been dropped off and/or needed a ride home. I didn't think any of it was a big deal. And telling the minister about my situation never entered my head.

This is another recurring thing in my life—not asking for help. I will sit there forever trying to figure something out before asking for help. I internalize it as my issue—I got myself into it, I can get myself out.

However, sometimes it's even deeper. I don't want to bother anybody, especially if there are others who need help too. The needs of others always outweighed my needs. I also equated self-care and being selfish. I think it is a very fine line to walk. A couple years ago, Terri had surgery. Before her surgery I was feeling really burned out. I needed to have some time to myself to recharge. I needed some self-care. The problem was I didn't know how to properly communicate what I needed. I think our friends were really concerned about how I would treat Terri during her recovery.

After her surgery, my alarm was set every 3.5 hours to ensure she had her meds and anything else she needed. I was there 24/7 and totally focused on her. I knew that is what I would do. A friend of mine had surgery and I stayed with her and did the same thing. I am a caretaker and I will give you everything I have to ensure your needs are met—as long as I am fully charged. Terri's pain was minimal and she understands now why I needed that time (hopefully so do our friends).

On another positive side, I believe problem solving is one of my strengths. Give me a problem and I will try to figure it out. I worked as a Bulk Mail Technician for the United States Postal Service for twelve out of thirty years. I worked at a printing company that sent semi-truck loads of mail every day. My job was to verify the mailings, bill them, and many times, order the trucks to move the mail. There was rarely a dull moment. Things came up and problems needed to be resolved. I was very good at my job.

How's that? I admitted I was good at something! Two positives in a row!

Outside of the office I had a great reputation. I had a great working relationship with those in higher positions. And I was respected for my knowledge and work ethic.

It wasn't the case with my co-workers and supervisors. There were a few I got along with very well, but most I didn't. I do take some responsibility, I had my moments when I was difficult. I went to war many times with management on the best way to do my job. They had no clue and didn't care. I poured myself into the job, gave it a thousand percent and it just wasn't good enough—sound familiar? I did have a postmaster and supervisor who listened to my concerns and worked with me. But my last couple of years that was not the case. They had moved on to greener pastures and the vultures came to rest. I can see where my past came into play as I repeatedly tried to get them to listen to me. It was a struggle. The continuing struggle to be heard and believed.

There were also things going on behind my back that I didn't know about—and that isn't going to the negative—I was singled out on a few occasions. A couple of my co-workers thought it was important for any new person coming out to work with me, to know I was a lesbian. The first person who was sent out started talking right away about how his daughter was a lesbian and how much he loved her partner, etc. I thought it was kind of odd since this was the first time I met him, however I appreciated him sharing with me. The second person who came out was more direct and told me what was going on. She was not happy with the other two co-workers. One of her very best friends was gay so there was no issue with her. Neither one of us could understand why they felt the need to inform people of my sexual preference. That's all I'm going to say about the post office unless something relevant comes up. It's thirty years of my life that doesn't need to be revisited here.

Not being heard however, is a struggle and a recurring issue. I do get upset when I'm not heard—I am slowly making progress. I remember dating someone and telling them something I was going to do. Their reply was "Okay." I kept repeating the same thing to them and they kept saying "Okay." I finally had to take a minute and sit there. They heard me the first time and acknowledged what I was going to do. They didn't push back or argue they just said, "Okay." It was a totally different experience for me. It was weird.

Going back to perception being reality, I talked with my therapist about the basketball game where I started and played great right away and how when I was pulled, I felt defeated. Her take was the coach recognized my effort and was just giving me a break and nothing more. But because I was usually only pulled when I messed up, it was a different experience for me and I went right to the negative. I did the same thing during my brief time as a sportswriter. I took editing as a negative instead of a learning experience.

I wonder how long I will keep going to the negative. I'm always surprised when people like me or talk to me. If people ignore me, I go right into that place of not being worthy. My comfort zone of sorts.

One place in my life I feel the knot loosen is my relationship with Terri. We are both getting better at communicating. When I feel she is upset with me, I straight up ask her—this is something new for me to do. Most of the time she is struggling with something not related to me and apologizes and lets me know what is happening. I used to internalize that and wonder what I did wrong and try to fix it—I try to fix something I have no idea what it even is. Some of that is the problem solver in me. Anyway, when the issue *is* about something I did, we are getting better about talking things out.

I feel sorry for Terri sometimes. I feel she tiptoes around me because she doesn't want to hurt me by telling me things that bother her. We are getting better trying to figure out how to communicate through this mental illness stuff. I'm not sure if we will ever figure it all out, however we definitely have a better understanding.

Sports

A quick side note.

For as long as I can remember my family has been involved in some way with sports. At my Grandma Kelsey's house we played softball and volleyball. My uncle even maintained a grass volleyball court complete with permanent poles and boundary lines. I don't remember it being about competition, it was about fun.

It wasn't until I got older that I started losing my confidence and not feeling good enough. Did I start comparing myself to my peers? When did the transformation happen? New thoughts. New things to talk with my therapist about.

I played volleyball in college and most of my adult life—indoor and outdoor. I played summer softball for many years including picking it back up in my late forties. I coached junior varsity basketball and was an assistant varsity coach. I ran elementary after school sports programs, helped coach my daughter's softball team and had a sixth grade traveling basketball team.

Why am I bringing this up? I don't know. Maybe I wanted to give as many girls as I could a positive sports experience? I wasn't perfect, but I tried to make it as inclusive as possible. I wanted every player to feel they mattered. They belonged. Perhaps I was trying to heal the broken child inside of me.

And I finally did have that basketball game I started back in high school. Basketball leagues, especially for women, were not easy to find. I was asked to play on one with players from my softball team. And I had *that* game. No matter how ugly or off balanced my shot was, it went in. I just played my heart out and thoroughly enjoyed the game. I scored 26 points.

I never thought of that before until today. It took about five years, but I finished something I had started at seventeen. The fear, anxiety, and unworthiness were nowhere to be found. I just played the game.

Maybe that is my new mantra—just play the game. Go out and enjoy it. Do what you love with total focus. Wrap yourself in that feeling of belonging and joy and let your being sing. Let your being soar....

Just play the game.

The Fairy Garden

Tending the weeds.

A couple years ago I started a fairy garden. It has been a fun hobby as I am learning and finding new things to do. One day a friend came to my house and I asked her if she wanted to see the fairy garden. Imagine my surprise when we walked over there and it was overgrown with weeds. I was shocked! How could that happen?

I was so embarrassed by how much it was overgrown and frantically started pulling weeds wondering how this could happen? The answer was simple; I stopped tending to it.

I realize I do that in a number of things in my life. A high school friend lived with me for a while. He had a job where he traveled and needed a place to land for a few days at a time. Before he moved in, we had hung out a couple times and went to a concert and a farmers market. After he moved in we did nothing. Not because of him, but because of me. He was looking forward to doing things when he came back—even simple things like watching "Glee" on TV. But I did nothing. I sat on the couch, watched TV, and played on the computer while he spent time in another room watching TV.

I do this in relationships too. Fall in love, move in, and detach. I guess it's like the other things, good enough to get to the first step, but can't follow through. Although this doesn't just affect my life, it affects another person too.

But why do I detach? Is it because I don't think I deserve being loved?

Probably. They were going to leave me someday because there was no way they could continue to love me. Sometimes I would go overboard with generosity and shower people with gifts and pay for things I could not afford. It was a distraction—look over here and look over there, but don't look at me because you really don't want me. Luckily I believe that behavior IS in the past. I learned the hard way financially you really cannot buy love.

Relationship-wise I am in a good one. I have a great partner. We aren't perfect and we don't strive for perfection. We just want to be happy and enjoy life and each other. It is a good place to be and it took a very long time for us to find it. And also luckily she has patience and is willing to try to understand the things I go through. I send her mixed messages a lot and we try to sort through them.

Six years ago when I retired from my first job, I moved to Milwaukee and bought a house. The house is a temporary stop before our final destination, closer to my daughter. I bought it partially as in investment. I put some good money into remodeling, but I left a lot of my things unpacked. I felt like I was straddling two lives—one where I came from and one where I was going. Neither were about where I actually was. I put off unpacking a lot of things and literally making myself at home. I kept saying, when we move I will get a new bed, set up an office, etc. I didn't want to get too invested emotionally in the house—or the neighbors— because I was moving soon. I was detaching.

I'm good at being a recluse. If it wasn't for work, I probably would have never left the house. When I had my "good six months" I was running, going to the athletic club, going to meetings, and had no problem taking day trips to go hiking. I was tending the garden of life and reaping the rewards of being present. I let the sun shine on my face and felt the warmth of living life. But that was the exception, not the rule. I lived in my last house for eight years and knew my neighbors mostly in passing. There were no get-togethers or hanging out. I kept to myself.

Things haven't work that way here. We've gotten to know our neighbors pretty well and enjoy our time together. If it wasn't for Terri and Covid, I probably would have kept mostly to myself because getting invested in people hurts when you leave. So if I didn't get to know them, it wouldn't hurt as much.

The houses on both sides have young children, so I did the what-kind-of-neighbor-would-I-want-if-I-had-young-children thing and we put a bridge in our landscaping so the families had easy access through the backyards. During Covid we would be sitting in the backyard and watched as the parents met to hand-off children and report on the day. Many afternoons we had informal gatherings on our front yard so the adults could talk and the kids could ride bikes on the sidewalk. We thoroughly enjoy our neighbors and are so grateful for them. What started as tender seedlings have grown into strong plants with strong roots. We will be in each other's lives long after our move.

Terri brings me to the present when I start to hibernate and stay inside on the couch with my tablet watching TV. We have made ourselves a beautiful outdoor oasis in the summer and I really enjoy sitting out there—once I get there. It is both calming and energizing. I love playing in the dirt planting and pulling weeds. I love all the different pots and flower arrangements. But again, sometimes I struggle to get out there. This past summer was very challenging, more on that later, but it shouldn't stop me from completely enjoying things I love. Is it the guilt of not feeling I deserve what I have? What makes me so special to have these things?

When Covid hit I needed to work from home on occasion. It forced me to make my home office a better place to work. Eventually I set it up to be a comfortable place to write. I didn't want to though. I didn't want to get comfortable. So now I have an office that feels good and has good vibes—I can actually feel it calling to me when I walk by it. And I try to ignore it. Fear of success? Fear of doing something for myself? I might actually get something done if I spend time in my office writing. Sigh, crazy thoughts.

So back to our topic. Why did I detach from my friend from school? It was just a friendship. I don't know. Perhaps I was playing the rescuer? I saw a friend in need and went to the what-do-I-wish-would-happen-if-I-was-in-this-situation mode. That's a possibility. I reached out and helped and then thought my job was done. I talked with my therapist about this and she agreed. I did my part to help someone out and I didn't think they would need anything else from me. I thought about that, what else would they want from me? I have nothing else to offer someone. Interesting. I cleared the weeds, gave him a place to land and then just withdrew. I expected him to tend to himself. I was no longer needed.

I just don't understand why I do these things. I missed a year of hanging out with someone and just withdrew from life.

We all have friends we don't see or talk with often, but when we have contact, it's like time stood still. We pick right up where we left off. These friendships have been fully cultivated and tended to over time. There are no weeds growing here.

It's not the same for all friendships and definitely not relationships. We need to tend the flowers and pull the weeds. We need to plant and harvest to grow. If we do nothing, the weeds will consume us.

I just had the thought that it is like doing chores. If we keep up on them a little at a time, they remain manageable. It's when we become overwhelmed with the weeds, all we can see are the weeds and feel there is no hope.

There is hope. When we feel we are being dragged down and choked by the weeds, we need to look up and find the sun. The sun will give us hope to move forward. It's not always easy, however there is always hope.

Dream Weaver

Did I dream that or did it happen?

There was a time in my life when my brain worked overtime. I think the term for it now is gaslighting. It is hard to live with someone who has a different reality than you or is it called alternate facts?

I am going to be careful here and only talk about my reality and how it affected me. There were many times when I saw things with my own eyes and the person I was with said it never happened. The same when we traveled. I told them to turn right, they turned left and blamed it on me. These things happened over and over.

My brain worked hard to keep me sane. I knew what happened and it was no use trying to get the other person to see the truth. They also never apologized or admitted they were wrong. One time there was a situation where something was misplaced and I was blamed for the missing object. When the object was found a few weeks later, it was clear that the other person was the one responsible for it missing. When I asked for an apology, I was told, "No, it's something you would have done."

I started to have stroke-like symptoms and had both a MRI and a MRA done, but nothing was found. I had two episodes of slurred speech and struggling to find words. The first episode lasted a few days, the other lasted a couple weeks. I finally made the excruciating decision to walk away. I felt that if I stayed longer, I would literally go crazy and end up in the psych ward. There were many other factors, however, to protect myself and others, this is all I am willing to share.

In the midst of it all, I had very real and vivid dreams. So not only was I struggling with trying to live in reality, sometimes I wasn't sure if something really happened or I dreamt it. I ran an after-school sports program at a local grade school. One day the principal called me into the office to tell me there was no more funding for the program and this was my last one. The next day, I submitted paperwork for the next round of activities—I could not remember if we really had the conversation or if it was a dream. She called me in to remind me of our conversation.

Some of you may relate and some of you may be wondering if I was the one who remembered things correctly. I remembered things correctly. How can I be sure? That's a great question. There were times when my anxiety was so high and I was so stressed it's like I blacked out. I didn't always remember how things and what things happened. It was scary sometimes. This was not the case. The incidents I remembered did not happen during a time of stress, they were everyday occurrences. They were incidents that I saw or heard and then I was told they didn't happen. Or I knew something was going on and it was denied over and over and then finally the truth came out and I was right. The other person would conveniently forget things that were either uncomfortable, embarrassing or their fault—they had no faults. And my reality didn't change. This is the best I can explain it.

After the relationship was over that person went to therapy. Months later they called me and told me what they had learned about themselves and actually, for the first time, acknowledged what had happened and apologized. It was sad. It was something that I had wanted to happen months and years ago. I begged to go to therapy together. I tried and tried until I could no longer try. I was happy for them and their discoveries. I was sad it took ending our relationship for it to happen. What is even more sad is when they became involved in another relationship, all of a sudden the truth was buried. We were back to the beginning where those things never happened.

Now back to our regularly scheduled program... The times I was stressed, or maybe feeling uncomfortable, yes, I think that is more correct.

Situations where I felt I needed to deflect and distract—be the entertainer to keep people at arm's length—were also times I was not fully in the presence of what was happening. One time I spilled a secret about a surprise party for a cousin. I honestly did not remember being told it was a secret. My mind was racing in a million other directions at the time and I did not fully remember the conversation.

This isn't limited to my adult years. I don't remember a lot about kindergarten, first and second grades. I can't tell you who my teachers were (except kindergarten) or who my friends were. My mom said I would grab someone's sack lunch and walk around the room asking who it belonged to. Why did I do that? I do remember a few things about kindergarten, however between kindergarten and first grade is when I was sexually abused by the hired hand. Is that why I did the things I did and also remember very little? Another thing to untangle and ask my therapist about.

I am better at staying in the present now. I don't feel the need to twist and turn myself into whatever makes those around me more comfortable. Like me or not. That's your choice. And it allows me to stay more focused around people.

I am also better at believing I am a likeable person and letting people know me—as much as I know me. I'm getting there, it's a process. Part of the process is not caring. If someone doesn't like me, so what? I also have the choice of not being around people. These are cases where those memes can be true. If you trigger me, I will not be around you. It's not worth going down the rabbit hole. It's called setting boundaries and some people do not like boundaries. And that's okay too.

I still have the vivid dreams, only they are weird enough for me to know they were dreams. I'm talking "Jumanji" weird—the first movie. It was really hard for me to watch that movie. Those things that happened also happened in my dreams. Sometimes I will have a run of violent dreams. I don't like those and find it hard to go to bed at night. For years and years I was not able to dial 911 in my dreams—on a rotary phone. Now I can—still on a rotary phone—but either no one answers or they tell me I have to call the emergency number.

Okay enough of that. I could write a whole book just about my dreams and try to find their representation in my life.

I'm just relieved to know they are dreams.

Relationships

Becoming ourselves.

I never really learned how to be in a relationship. I dated a little in high school and had a serious relationship where instead of going away to college, I stayed in the area and went to college. The plan was for me to go to college until he graduated from high school—he was younger. Then I would work while he went to college. And after he had a degree and a job, I would eventually go back to school. I put myself second because that's what you did. So in case you were wondering why I played volleyball in college instead of basketball, that is why. I went to a two-year college to get my associate degree and they had very few sports. I wanted to attend a school within the University of Wisconsin system instead of a private college—even though there were a couple in the area.

As many high school romances do, ours fizzled out. There were many reasons, however, I think there were two main reasons. One was just the fact he was trying to enjoy high school and I was trying to find my place in the world. I was working two jobs, going to school, and made the volleyball team. Maybe I was keeping busy so I didn't have to feel? I lived with my grandma so I had a home base and made new friends, however, I think I was lonely. I missed my family. I jumped into my new life without a lot of thought—or at least that is how it feels now. But I am glad I had that time with my grandma.

Secondly was my icky uncle. Some time during our dating is when it happened. Sometimes I wish I could remember exactly when it happened and how it changed me. But I don't. The only thing I remember is hanging out at my grandma's house with my college friends. I don't remember the conversation, but one of the guys made the comment, "Kim's putting on weight, but we still love her." This is one of those "blackout" periods in my life where I remember very little. The things I do remember, I cannot put in a definitive timeline.

I had an unhealthy relationship with love. There were a lot of mixed messages. I thought my parents had a pretty good relationship. They were equals and we were brought up as equals. Everyone did the same chores and had the same expectations—it didn't matter if you were female or male. I worked at a movie theater and saw a lot of movies—movies are so different now. One of my favorites was "Saturday Night Fever," but watching it now is a lot different. It makes me cringe to see how women were treated. Society pressed upon us that other females were our enemies and males were the ultimate prize. You were to do anything and everything to keep a man. Sadly, there are still women out there who feel that way. They need a man to boost their self-worth. I had two friends who married badly. They both told me at different times, "A bad husband is better than no husband at all."

In a way, I did the same. I stayed in relationships because that is what you did—even if you were fighting for your sanity. You found your person and stayed with them forever—society and religion also influenced this thinking. You threw everything about you away to mold yourself around them. Yeah, I know that wasn't healthy, but neither was I.

I spent one relationship pretty much in a bar. It was the perfect relationship at the time—they liked to drink, I liked to eat. We didn't have to deal with a lot of reality because we were constantly distracting ourselves. I spent a lot of money on them and dug myself into a financial hole. But I had to. If I didn't give them everything they wanted, maybe they would not want me.

Yeah, that was *real* healthy. I'm not real comfortable hanging out in bars now. It brings back some unhealthy feelings, like the urge to order a ton of food. It can be triggering for me especially when people get drunk and obnoxious. When that happens, I want to leave. I was around that for three years and don't like to revisit it. That is when the fun stopped and I had to step in and be the adult, the caretaker. There was a point of no return and I knew when things were about to change. It wasn't fun. I have to be pretty spiritually fit to go and sit for hours. I don't drink a lot and there's only so much diet cola one can consume.

As I wrote that I realized I can sit on the couch for hours and do nothing. Unfortunately, that is my comfort zone—the unhealthy zone.

I was dating someone in early 2012 when I was starting to finally get myself together—remember those six months of success? With them I felt mixed messages. They wanted me to be healthy and when I got healthy it felt as though they were pushing me away. So I walked away. It was easier this time. Looking back I can see where their role in life is being a rescuer. I needed rescuing and when I started to thrive, I think it scared them. What would our relationship be like if I no longer needed to be rescued? We will never know.

I learned how to be alone and the difference between being alone and lonely. When I start feeling lonely I'm not really, I'm depressed. I start missing people and instead of reaching out, I dig myself into a hole. Poor me. No one loves me. No one wants to be around me. These are very dangerous and toxic thoughts.

Through it all, I am learning how to be myself in a relationship, which is tricky, as I am trying to figure out who *I* am! There is progress. There is hope. And there is Terri.

We are not perfect and sometimes we struggle. However the best thing is our relationship is built on trust. I don't have to worry about her flirting or cheating on me. When she goes out or away with friends, there is no anxiety or fear filling my head about what she might be doing. It is satisfying and comforting.

I feel like I am finally cracking that code of who I am in a relationship. Although she is a giver too. Being with a giver, when you were usually the one doing all the giving, takes some adjusting. We have a few things to figure out both together and separately, but we'll get there.

I remember while working the twelve steps in OA, step six is about removing our defects of character. Sometimes our character defects are where our comfort lays and if they are gone, who are we? Sigh, it's all a work in progress. We can't go into a relationship expecting the other person to change. And we also can't go into a relationship losing our identity.

Every chapter I write and every issue I encounter, I am learning. I am learning about who I am, why I do the things I do, or did or thought… I am becoming.

Hitting Rock Bottom

An unexpected summer.

I reread chapter "2023" and it was interesting how I was filled with such hope and optimism at the beginning of this year. My second grandchild was born in February, a beautiful sweet little boy. My granddaughter wasn't real happy—she wanted a sister and didn't like his name. However, it didn't take long before she was in love with him. I think it took a little longer for her to forgive her parents, but she got there.

After I came home from my first visit with my daughter and family, I caught a cold and it was mainly in my throat. It was the end of February and as I do with most things, I put it off—I mean, if it's not Covid then it's okay. Well, not this time.

I traveled to Georgia in March where I met up with my mom, dad, Terri, and my daughter and her family. We had a great time and I pushed through with the cold. By the time we left Georgia, the cold had moved into my eyes. Shortly after returning home, I woke up one morning with both eyes matted shut. Okay, now things are getting serious, time to contact a doctor. I was given antibiotics for my eyes and they cleared up, however, the cold in my throat was still there. I went to urgent care and they did all the tests, x-rays, breathing treatments, and gave me some antibiotics. This was the end of April.

I started to notice little blisters in my hair and behind my ears and by June, I had blisters over a significant portion of my body.

The best we can piece together is this, I got a topical yeast infection from the antibiotics, on my head. When the weather heated up, being a heavy person, any skin fold that retained moisture broke out to a blistering rash. Now as a heavy person, I have dealt with heat rashes, so I was pretty certain I could handle it. Nope. Not even a little. I was visiting my daughter when it all came crashing down. Dramatic? Probably. Life changing? Definitely.

By the time I went to the doctor, they had determined I had a topical yeast infection with a secondary bacterial infection. I had ointments and meds—one antibiotic and one for yeast infection.

I was miserable and at a pain level I could never imagine. I felt bad for my daughter, I was up there to help her family and they ended up helping me. How I made it back home is a miracle. It is a seven-hour drive and I had to stop halfway and stay overnight.

I spent most of the summer wrapped in sheets, because clothing hurt, and stayed inside most days. Heat, sweat and anything tight was not my friend. I was miserable. Things were clearing up slowly and my pain level was becoming tolerable. In the early stages I wanted to be put in a medical coma because the pain was so severe.

I felt I had hit my bottom. Not unlike an alcoholic who had nowhere else to go but up. I swore off sweets and was determined to lose weight—I never wanted to go through this pain again. Nothing tasted that good.

By the end of September things were clearing up and I had my annual physical with my primary doctor—this was the first time she knew any of this was happening. I had two biopsies and blood tests that went to Mayo. Things were ruled out, but there are no definite answers on what was happening. The blisters have never fully gone away.

I missed out on a lot of things, including the simple joy of pulling weeds and playing with the plants. I could only tolerate things so long before I had to take a shower and put medication on my blisters.

I missed spending time with my daughter and getting to know my grandson. I missed playing disc golf and had lost so much stamina.

I started doing online OA meetings and enjoyed connecting with people and working the steps. I was determined to be better—to live. I wanted to live. I was writing and making some good progress on my first book. I was making good life choices too and losing weight.

Every time I finished a chapter, I was excited and actually a little impressed with myself. I wasn't going to make the self-imposed deadline of August, however I was getting there. I can do this. I CAN do this!

I felt the hope and optimism of 2023. I could have easily gone down the rabbit hole of depression and anxiety, but I worked to keep moving forward. Just a little bit every day, every hour. I can do this.

Chapter Ten

The pause.

Nope. Here we go again. Whereas October was productive and filled with hope, it changed in November. I have written very little this month. My first book is coming along well even though my self-imposed August deadline for completion has passed.

Sometimes I think I'm going crazy. So many mixed emotions and feelings. I was focused on health and feeling better and then it just switches off.

I think what is really happening could be the same ole same ole. I start to have success and then stop. I'm down thirty-five pounds, but I'm eating sweets again and stopped doing OA meetings.

I was working on Chapter Ten and I stopped. It's a good book. I have a writing coach who gives me edits and positive feedback.

But I stopped.

I was talking with Terri and told her, "I think I'm done writing 'Making Russian Dolls.'" She was shocked. I said, "Well, it's going good, and I know I can do it." The words she said next were very, very insightful, "Yes you can do it, but you have never finished."

Whoa, she is right. It's like most things in my life, I start, things go good and I stop. I don't follow through. I have done this with so many things in my life, including people. The list is very long.

So where do I go from here? I don't know.

My goal was to have one book published by the end of 2023 and this one ready to go right behind it in early 2024. Am I a failure? Was this summer an excuse?

It's a good thing I retired from my second job in May. I did it with the intention of writing full-time, but could not find the structure. I also would have been out most of the summer with my health issues. I could not wear clothes, let alone sit at a desk for hours.

I decided to take a pause from Chapter Ten and concentrate on this book. Maybe it will help me get back on track. Who knows, maybe this one will get published first? Or will I get a really good start and stop? And then go back to the other one?

All this is going through my brain. I need to get it out. Purge. The self-doubt, anxiety, fear, depression—all my traveling companions—are fighting for the wheel and I am in the trunk gasping for air…

…and we're heading for a cliff…

The Universe and James Patterson

My unofficial mentors.

My whole life, I felt like I was here to help the world and writing books felt like a selfish endeavor. While writing skits and plays for the church felt like a calling, I struggled at taking compliments. "It's not me, it's God," I would say. I felt guilty if I took joy in what I did.

Times when I struggled the Universe gave me encouragement. Some meme would pop up on Facebook or there was a news story about a woman who accomplished her dreams at a later stage of life. I took them all as a message to continue to move forward. I still struggled with the "selfishness" of writing, who was that helping? Then came James Patterson.

I was watching *Morning Joe* and James Patterson and Mike Lupica were on promoting their joint novel. During the interview James said something to the effect of, "With the state of the world, people need a distraction from reality. Reading books helps people escape."

It hit me like a ton of bricks. There was my answer—my purpose. My books might not save the world, however they could give people a relief, an escape from reality. It was both a welcome thought and slightly sad one—I mean if writing was indeed the answer I have been looking for and asking the Universe, what will be my excuse for not continuing to write?

This was a powerful message for me. Writing and wanting to share my talent with the world is not a selfish gesture. It is my contribution, my offering to the world.

Thank you James Patterson.

Again

Or is it still?

When I fully retired I no longer had a schedule or structure. Although I was struggling with my health, I could do *something,* but I was feeling a little lost. It felt similar to those times when I was so overwhelmed with chores to do, I couldn't do any. Now I had so much time to do anything I wanted and didn't know where to start. So I did nothing.

I contacted a friend for help. I felt I needed an "accountability coach"—someone for additional support. I wanted someone to report my progress to everyday, someone I looked up to. I was struggling on keeping a schedule and if I stopped for any reason, it could be a long time before I started again. I chose a person I wished had been in my life when I was younger. She would have been a great mentor and is someone I look up to. One thing I appreciate about her is I can ask her any question and she doesn't make me feel stupid. She listens and responds with patience as I try to understand.

I had been thinking about focusing my writing on this book and take a step back from my other book "Making Russian Dolls." Although I was ten chapters and over a hundred pages in, I felt like my brain was full and I had to get some stuff out of it. Writing in this book would help sort out some feelings I was having with this journey. However I had to be sure the decision wasn't driven by my pals fear and anxiety. I was having success and things were progressing well—was I falling back into old habits?

When I expressed my thoughts to my friend she asked, "Why don't you work on it?" I weirdly needed someone to say it out loud. I wanted validation about a decision I had made. I think perhaps it was because I am not quitting my other book, I am *pausing* it. And after I am done writing this book, I might need a gentle push to continue.

I think after my conversation with Terri about never finishing something, I want to assure myself I would indeed be moving on and not stopping for months—old unhealthy behavior.

Okay, so when I finally switched my focus to this book, my writing took off like crazy! I was easily doing over one thousand words in two hours. I was shocked. Unlike my other book, this is just "pure" writing— whatever enters my brain and comes out of my fingers. I was amazed at how fast things were coming out and going together. And……. the brakes came on. I found myself waiting later and later to write. HOWEVER, reporting to my friend did keep me writing! Well, most days. I didn't write one day, but it was only one day and did not lead into several as it would have previously. One step in the right direction!

My friend's role is similar to a twelve-step sponsor. We started with a plan of action which included sending her a message at the end of the day whether I accomplished my goal. It's not like she can discipline me and there are no consequences for not following through. But in the back of my brain I kept thinking I don't want to disappoint her. I think what I'm really saying is I don't want to disappoint ME. She has no skin in the game. She does not profit in any way. However, I think that knowing she is there, has helped me keep going.

After we had been doing this for a week, I wanted to rethink things. I started going down that rabbit hole—things were progressing nicely, but I was feeling pressure. Talking with my "coach" had me thinking about a lot of things. There was no right or wrong way on how to do this—it was new territory for me. And the only timeline was the self-imposed one I put upon myself. I felt I had to sit down and do so many hours a day. Why? I just felt I needed to do it. But *why*? Was I subconsciously setting myself up for failure? I was feeding my anxiety and fear while starving my soul. Whoa, I kind of like that thought. I mean, not *really* like it, but it resonates.

When I feed those life passengers, I starve my soul. And many times when my soul is starving, I overfeed my body. Wow, wow, wow. I think I should start highlighting my new insights so I can reference them. I am going to have a lot to talk about with my therapist! The only thing I really needed to do was find out what works for *me*.

I had struggled with setting a schedule for writing. I talked to my Higher Power seeking answers. I worked hard for people/businesses for forty-seven years. Why can't I work hard for myself? Don't I deserve it? I don't like the words "I deserve." I don't feel like I *deserve* anything. Why would I deserve something when there are people struggling? Don't they deserve something too?

These are just some thoughts that enter my mind. I think I have settled on telling myself "I have earned this." It feels softer. I have earned time in my life to stop working for others and work for myself. I have earned time in my life to do what I want to do and learn who I am. I have earned time in my life to express my creative self. For me. If other people like what I'm doing, it's a bonus. I have earned this.

I struggle with success and progress. Well I struggle with a lot of things. I told Terri if our friend ever calls her up concerned about my thought process, she interrupted me and said, "Welcome to my world." Oh so true.

Some people don't like the word crazy and the insinuations associated with the word. But that's how I feel sometimes. There are a million things going on in my head and I either can't get them out or they all spill out and make no sense.

Even though this book isn't one that will help the world escape reality, I hope if one person reads this and feels some comfort in knowing they are not alone, this will all be worth it. I hope my words and experiences can help someone. And maybe those who are living with someone like me, will have some insight.

It's not a fun place to be and I think that is why I prefer to play games on my tablet and watch TV. It's a distraction from reality. I don't have to think. My fellow travelers and I are in a RV. They are taking turns driving and I am sitting comfortably in the back unaware of where we are going.

Until I look up and see we are going over a cliff. That's how it feels when I procrastinate too long and put things off. It's like it's too late to do anything about it now. That's why I am grateful I am reporting to my friend. I have time to grab the wheel and get back on track. None of it is easy. And all of it is easy. See why I think I'm crazy? I think if I close my eyes and look into my brain, it will be swirling around like a tornado.

Another thing I do is set high expectations, it's almost like self-sabotage. The weird thing is if I meet those expectations, not only am I shocked, but feel compelled to stop. I find excuses to stop—none of which are actual reasons. A reason for me can be after a therapy session, sometimes I have what I call emotional hangovers. I need to have some quiet time to absorb and process the feelings. Being sick is a reason. Being tired can be both a reason and an excuse.

Sometimes an obstacle is there for us to turn away from and go another direction. Other times an obstacle is there for us to work through and learn from. When I hit an obstacle, real or perceived, I need to take time to look for the answer and RECEIVE the answer.

When I moved to Milwaukee and bought my house, it was a very tedious process. Being retired there were a few hoops to jump through to satisfy the credit union. Many times I wondered if the Universe was sending me a message I shouldn't buy a house. After I met all the criteria for the loan, found and had an accepted offer on a house, it came to a stop. The sellers had a few issues on their hands they needed to clear up. Both my realtor and a friend in the loan business, told me I should look for something else. We were supposed to move in around Christmas, but it was put on an indefinite hold.

I stopped looking at houses. I had my heart set on this one and couldn't bring myself to continue looking. So I thought I would just take a break until spring and look again. But I still had my hopes on this one.

It all came together and we moved in in February! All and all I was happy I didn't quit. Many times at the smallest obstacle I would stop and not continue, this time I made it through. I was very drained and stressed. But I did it. It was a good lesson for me. When I hit an obstacle now, I really have to look at it and ask the Universe if this is something I need to work through or make a U-turn and do something different.

The other day I told my friend I wasn't going to write. I mean it was eleven o'clock at night. There wasn't any reason, I just procrastinated the whole day. Now if I had been busy doing things and ran out of time, that would be a reason. My friend said, "Okay, but maybe commit to five days weekly." I keep notes on a calendar of my progress. Sure enough, I had only worked three days. Fine. Sigh… I got up and went to my office and wrote until after two o'clock in the morning. I don't mind staying up late at night. It's quiet, the house is asleep and I am alone in my thoughts.

Being alone in my thoughts can be a blessing and a curse. The subtitle of this book says it all—ramblings from a chaotic mind. My writing process is much different in this book. I just sit down and spew out everything going through my brain. This book will probably need a lot of editing for it to have some kind of flow. I am trying to do some as I go along. My other book requires a lot more thought and some research to be reasonably accurate. It also has a lot of dialogue. All in all it takes a few hours to get over a thousand words written.

Although, as I have learned, editing makes things better. Hmmm… is there a life editor?

The Knot

Part two.

Right now, at this very moment, I am feeling good about how this book is coming along. I no longer feel I am straddling between finishing and not finishing.

I recently visited my daughter and I was not planning on writing. I made hard copies to work on instead of bringing the laptop—I find it easier to edit by making notes that way. What I didn't do was communicate to my accountability coach what my intentions were. We were still navigating some unfamiliar territory.

I also had taken the copies to my therapy appointment and talked to my therapist about some things I was struggling to understand and things I had unearthed. When I asked my accountability coach if that counted as working on the book, her response was, "That is up to you. I would think if it moves the book forward it counts some."

Those words were like a spark of energy. I didn't need to spend a lot of time working on it while I was visiting. Just doing something to move it forward was a great idea. I didn't do a lot of editing, however, I did start taking notes and outlining new chapters.

My accountability coach had concerns though, I might be slipping. We had a very productive chat. I told her in the past, I would not have done anything at my daughter's—or very little—and when I returned home I would continue to do nothing.

This is all a learning process for me and I am not seeking perfection—first of all I have no idea what that even looks like. I'm seeking progress. If I work on my writing a little each day, whether writing, researching or editing, any of it is better than nothing.

The biggest thing I am learning is to not put so much pressure on myself by adding deadlines and goals. I do think that one hour is reasonable for a minimum starting point. One hour a day is not much time when you consider I can literally sit on the couch all day doing nothing.

Structure is different than timelines. I need to establish a schedule. All my life I had schedules and deadlines, whether it was work or going to bed as a child. So when I retired for the last time to start my new adventure of writing, I was now working for myself. I was the boss. And I didn't have to do anything if I didn't want to. Ugh. That was not the correct way to think, because all I wanted to do was hang out on the couch and do nothing. Enlisting a friend as an accountability coach has added a little structure, but I have a lonnnnnng way to go. In writing that last sentence I had a Freudian slip. I originally typed in accountability *couch* instead of *coach*. It would be easy to use her as a couch instead of a coach. After all, how does she really know I am giving her the correct information and really doing what I say I am doing? And that is exactly why I asked her to be my coach. I respect her too much to not tell the truth. I'm also learning to respect myself and lying is not an easy thing for me to do. It eats me up inside and is not worth it.

This chapter in my life is new and I can't do it by myself right now. I need affirmation and accountability. I feel the knot changing from a small rigid metal knot into a bigger rope one. One that can be more easily unraveled. The words "the travel unraveled" just popped into my brain. Not sure what it means, but I like it. Perhaps it is the further I travel down the road in processing, learning, and getting myself together, the more the knot unravels.

The Pandemic

More casualties than we know.

Like many people, I had friends who died of Covid-19. This is not a chapter about politics, conspiracy theories or any of that stuff. It doesn't belong in this book. This chapter is about the toll it took on people's mental health and how it affected mine.

The first time I went into a grocery store it was surreal. There were markings on the floor to direct traffic and where to stand to maintain a six foot distance. The store was as vacant as the shelves. Some items had a limit on how many could be bought.

Shortly after walking in, I felt an anxiety attack coming on. I walked by the seasonal items and saw a plush pig—one of my favorite animals—and I grabbed it up and walked around the store hugging it to my chest. I made it through the store and home, holding the pig the whole time—only surrendering it briefly to be scanned at the register. Once settled, I broke down crying.

Why did this happen? No clue really. The world had changed and no one knew where things were going for certain. Facebook had become a war zone for everyone's views and of course I felt I needed to get my opinion out there. I was scared. I think that was the bottom line for me. I didn't want any more friends dying and certainly didn't want any family—or children—to die. I fell into that old trigger of not being heard and kept after those with different views. Why aren't you listening to me! I wasn't always pleasant about voicing my opinion.

And then I found Grub Hub and Door Dash, the absolute worst thing for someone with a food addiction. If I ordered out, I didn't have to go to the grocery store and it was helping the area restaurants. An excuse or a reason? I didn't even have to open the door to see the delivery person, they just dropped it on the doorstep—it was heavenly.

Even though I had to leave the house for work, things had changed. Many times I was the only one in the office. Traffic was minimal. People were nasty on the phones. I think people forgot they were talking to another human being and took out all of their frustrations on us. It was a difficult time.

Anxiety and fear were more prevalent than ever and in full control. Depression was happily dancing around enjoying it all. I didn't want to go anywhere or do anything and well, I couldn't really do anything.

When things started to change slightly I was extremely careful on what I chose to do. Whereas previously I would do things by myself, this was no longer the case. I analyzed over and over any situation before I decided to go. I had developed "friend pods"—small groups of people I would do things with who I felt were safe. I didn't realize it then, but now I can see how I surrounded myself with like-minded people that I felt "safe" around. What I mean about "safe" is if I was to start struggling, having a panic attack or something similar, I knew these people would have my back. They would be supportive and sympathetic and I would not have to worry about being ridiculed or demeaned. They were my shields.

It has taken a toll on me. Whereas before I loved meeting up with people and going to parties, now it is very hard. I learned I can't think about it, I just have to get up and go. The longer I think about the upcoming event, the more I struggle to go—especially if I am going by myself.

It has taken a toll on my family. I miss them. We stopped having family gatherings and it seems there is more that divides us now than will bring us together.

New Year's Day I was going with Terri to meet up with her friends and watch the Badger game. We always have a fun time when we get together and it had been a long time since I saw them. But the closer it got, the more hesitant I became. I didn't want to sit in a bar… well… I didn't want to go out.

Other than my pals fear and anxiety, there is no logical reason—or excuse—for not going. Sigh, another thing to talk about with my therapist. My comfort zone is staying home, inside and ignoring the world. It is also the most unhealthiest zone and the one that feeds my traveling companions. Maybe that is it? Could it be I happily hand over the steering wheel to them as an excuse to stay home?

I miss that Kim. The one who just goes out and enjoys life. But then again, was I really out enjoying it or hiding behind the smiley face mask like in those commercials? Covid helped me become more and more comfortable with staying inside and not venturing out. It has become a tug of war in my soul. Or is it a tug of war *for* my soul?

I have allowed a pandemic to have control over my life. Again, this is not political or conspiracy filled. It is the fear, anxiety, and death that filled the Universe and found a place in me. It's like it sensed a vulnerability and came straight at me. I never thought of it like that before.

Terri and I are hoping to do more day trips this year. Covid is here to stay and I have to find a way to keep the fear and anxiety in check. Funny isn't it? I spent time talking about wanting to die, but not in my hands and here is something that could have taken me down and I tried like hell to avoid it.

When I mentioned day trips I could feel my heart starting to sing. I love being outside—I LOVE being outside. But I have allowed my traveling companions to keep me inside where *their* comfort zone is. If I spend time outside, it literally directs sunshine to my soul. My traveling companions don't want that. They want the rot to continue. They want to continue bringing me down so they can feed on me. And when they bring me down, depression will consume me.

Karma

Not necessarily bad.

This is a short read about karma. It doesn't have to be bad. We put things out in the Universe and the Universe in return replies in kind, or not so kind.

Despite all my flaws and character defects, I believe in my core, my soul, I am a good person. Didn't see that coming did ya? Neither did I. I try to do random acts of kindness whenever I can. I will be doing something and I get a spark from the Universe, a message of sorts. I can feel it in my soul and follow through. You never know what a person is going through or their struggles and one act of kindness can make all the difference. I just helped a lady tonight at the grocery store and I started crying. You don't need to know what I did, that will remain between me and the Universe. The point is she will remember the day someone was kind to her. Maybe she will pass it on to someone else. Or not. The Universe knows.

I didn't do it expecting anything or run home and put it on social media—just typing that makes me cringe. Perhaps the Universe needed a random act of kindness in all the heartbreak happening and I filled that void.

Whatever it is, it makes me cry and fills my soul.

And another soul is home tonight feeling special.

It's a Wonderful Life

It's just a little harder for some of us.

I was going to end this book with 2024 and all the dreams, plans, blah, blah, blah, until I started looking for the movie "It's a Wonderful Life." I have been watching it for the past ten years and it always hits me hard. I know what it feels like to wish you'd never been born.

An aunt of my mom's wanted her to have an abortion when she got pregnant with me. Abortion was illegal in the 1960s. I never understood why she was so unfriendly to me. She would glare at me during family gatherings. I learned about the pressure she had put on my mom much later. It explained a lot of things. I remember my dad telling me one time I was the only child that *had* been planned!

I think about what things could possibly look like in the world today if I did not exist. What would my family look like without me? Would my parents still have married? What about the people I dated or in a relationship with? Would my daughter still have been born? What about those random acts of kindness? Would those lives be different?

Maybe there was a reason I could not find that movie on TV this year. Sometimes that movie would take me down the darkest and saddest rabbit hole of all, no one would care if I died. That thought is absolutely not true. And again, I'm not talking about suicide, suicide is never the answer, it's a permanent "cure" for a temporary situation. I don't say those words lightly. A temporary situation could last for years. The pain inside caused by depression is hard to explain to someone who has never experienced it.

When I get to that darkest point, I run through in my head those who would not understand my absence, like my granddaughter and oddly my cats—especially my emotional support cat. They are innocents who do not understand how the world works and they would be heartbroken.

Of course there are others who would be heartbroken too and I don't mean to sound like I am dismissing their place in my life. They are the next ones on the mental list going through my brain. I keep running those people through my head over and over until I start feeling some relief. I wonder if I should include things that make me happy, like being outside. Fresh air and sunshine give me hope. I will have to think about that.

I'm telling you this as a tool that works for me. It helps me get out of the funk and try to face what is going on. And I don't always know what is going on and that's where, for me, therapy helps. I get validation and answers. I learn about what is happening and how to think about it differently. It's all about unraveling those knots and digging out the rot in our cores. There is no sense of putting good healthy stuff in our souls with old rotten stuff sticking to the bottom.

Medication can help too. Mine keeps me at a more even keel. Yes I still have my moments, but I can't imagine what they would be like if I didn't have help—in every aspect.

Thank you for going on this journey to somewhere with me. The second book I started writing and the first to be published. I have cleared out a lot of the rot and understand more than I ever expected.

You never know what someone is going through in their life. There is a saying "Hurt people, hurt people" and it is so true. I hope you have found some comfort in my experience. There is hope for all of us whether we are the ones dealing with mental illness personally or watching someone we love going through it. Whichever it is, be kind. Be kind to yourself. Be kind to others. I wish us all the hope of a wonderful life. Just play the game.

~~Writer's~~ Author's Notes

I was at a gathering with old and new friends. I walked into the kitchen and was asked "Did you find your muse?"

I looked at this new friend quizzically. "No?" I answered confused.

"Aren't you the writer?" She asked, now a little confused herself.

"I'm writing a book, actually two books."

"Were you downstairs writing?"

"No, I was just cooling off."

My new friend went on to ask me questions which I was hesitant to answer. Why was I reluctant to share information about my book(s)? The answer came more quickly than the question was formed—*because you are afraid. You are afraid you won't finish. You are afraid of failure. But mostly, you are afraid of succeeding.*

Stop it, my brain said. *You ARE doing it! It might be going slowly; however, you keep going. Your work is solid.*

But am I a writer? I asked myself.

This conversation stuck in my brain. Am I a writer? I feel being a writer is something that is earned *after* your book is published—or at least written. But then, would I not be an author? My book(s) were still in their infancy.

This was a dream I have had forever. Every place I lived, worked or visited, I always looked for a place to write. I always took a notebook and pen so I was able to write (sometimes the notebook remained blank). I have had stories and characters living in my brain for as long as I can remember. As a child, I wrote skits for my siblings to perform for the neighbors. As an adult, I wrote skits/plays/services for the church youth group (a dream fulfilled!). I was a sportswriter for a very brief time until my anxiety consumed me.

A dreamer dreams. A writer writes.

With the publication of this book, I can indeed call myself a writer. I was able to work through anxiety, and self-doubt. It took a lot to trust myself and trust my Higher Power's guidance. It is a humbling thought for me and one I feel I need to thank my *being* for hanging in there.

Sometimes when we step off that cliff, instead of falling, we find we are standing on solid ground. We didn't see it at first due to all the negative energy, anxiety, and self-doubt running through us.

Take that step. A dreamer can write and a writer can dream.

And in the end, a book becomes a reality… and a writer becomes an author.

This book is finished. I started and finished something.
The journey continues…

A Note to Lisa

You are the only one to see the words I wrote to show the world.

Where you saw strength, I felt weakness.

Where you felt hope, I saw darkness.

The tears I shed after our conversation, washed away the self-doubt

I felt in my soul.

When I remember to turn that prism of thoughts, just a little,

it can change my view.

It can allow the light of positivity and hope to flow through my mind

where darkness once lived.

Thank you for your honesty and guidance.

Thank you Lisa.

A Blistering Note

After this book was submitted for publication, the cause of the blisters was discovered. In the spring of 2023, the topical yeast infection caused my sugar levels to become high and inconsistent. I was put on a new medication. Unbeknownst to me, I was allergic to the medication. An allergic reaction had been considered, however, the focus was on laundry soap, clothing, sugar intake, etc., never the medication.

Although the dermatologist ruled me cured in early 2024, I was skeptical. I was still experiencing minor blistering. My primary physician agreed there was still an ongoing issue.

It all came to a head when I was told, due to high A1C, to double the medication I had been prescribed in spring of 2023. My blisters came roaring back. Terri did some research and found the answer—I was allergic to the medication. As of this writing, I still have a few that are popping up on my scalp, but all the others have healed.

I have a newfound appreciation for my body. It worked extremely hard to keep me alive for a year and I am grateful. My instincts for wanting to be hospitalized, were not too far off. And perhaps answers would have been found sooner rather than later—we'll never know for sure.

First Covid, then a severe allergic reaction. Either one could have been the answer I was searching for in my darkest moments. The Universe must want me to stay on earth a little longer.

I will embrace this newfound lease on life and lovingly embrace the body I hated for so long. I feel like there's a new beginning waiting around the corner for me. Maybe I can finally accept my body as an ally instead of an enemy. And perhaps with my body and mind working together, I can pack up those life passengers in a trunk and throw away the key.

Sounds like the beginning of a new book!